BELIEF,
being,
AND
BEYOND

About the Author

*"I am here to inspire, encourage, and
empower you to be your authentic self."*

Joy "Granddaughter Crow" Gray has received a BS in business management as well as a BS in business administration, an MBA, and a doctorate in leadership. She has several years of experience in corporate America working for an international company and additional time working for the government, and has worked as a college professor. She is here to share and serve under the name of Granddaughter Crow.

Internationally recognized as a Medicine Woman, Granddaughter Crow was born an empath and medium. She comes from a long lineage of spiritual leaders and esoteric wisdom. Raised by spiritual leaders, as a child she was fashioned and trained to serve the people through ministry. She is a member of the Navajo Nation (her father) and also has Dutch heritage (her mother). Granddaughter Crow provides a sense of integration through life experience.

Granddaughter Crow was inducted into the Delta Mu Delta International Honors Society in 2012, was voted Woman of the Year 2015 by the National Association of Professional Women (NAPW), and was featured in *Native Max Magazine*'s June/July 2016 issue.

In 2014, Granddaughter Crow founded the Eagle Heart Foundation, a 501(c)(3) nonprofit organization dedicated to charitable giving and educational enhancement for all cultures and populations for the purpose of honoring the ancestors and responding to their heartfelt prayers.

Granddaughter Crow ®

BELIEF,

being,

AND

BEYOND

Your Journey to Questioning Ideas, Deconstructing Concepts & Healing from Harmful Belief Systems

Granddaughter Crow

Llewellyn Publications | Woodbury, MN

FIRST EDITION
First Printing, 2022

Book design by Christine Ha
Cover design by Kevin R. Brown
Tarot card illustrations are from the Tarot Original 1909 Deck by Pamela Colman
    Smith and Arthur Edward Waite. Used with permission of Lo Scarabeo s.r.l.

Llewellyn Publications is a registered trademark of Llewellyn Worldwide Ltd.

Library of Congress Cataloging-in-Publication Data (Pending)
ISBN: 978-0-7387-7175-5

Llewellyn Publications
A Division of Llewellyn Worldwide Ltd.
2143 Wooddale Drive
Woodbury, MN 55125-2989
www.llewellyn.com

Printed in the United States of America

Other Books by Granddaughter Crow

The Journey of the Soul

Wisdom of the Natural World

Contents

FOREWORD

As a youth, Granddaughter Crow tells us that she was taught not to question.

Thank God she didn't listen.

If she had, we never would have received, in the pages of this book, answers to two of life's ultimate questions: Who are we? And what lies beyond? "Approach life with curiosity and ask questions, for it is the only way to gain answers," she implores us.

This entire book is one grand question. Profound. Simple. Elegant.

Granddaughter Crow uses her innate curiosity and intelligence to construct a radical new cognitive framework for understanding the mysteries of the complex Universe in which we live.

Belief, Being, and Beyond is wonderfully unique in that it encompasses the views and perspectives of seemingly disparate belief systems to create a foundational new paradigm for understanding cultural perspectives. What does Christianity have in common with the tarot? What does Paganism have in common with

Navajo creation stories? What does Jesus have in common with the Hindu deity Manu? Read on. Granddaughter Crow will enlighten you to the fact that there is far more that unites our varied human systems of belief than we may have ever considered.

Combining indigenous wisdom with a pointed focus on the power of the cycles of the natural world, you'll learn what season of life you're currently existing in (spring, summer, autumn, or winter), as well as what energies and direction on the medicine wheel you are moving into (becoming). In exploring such questions, you'll be a wiser, more well-rounded person who knows how to naturally *be* with the rhythms of life rather than fruitlessly swimming upstream.

Taking great care not to judge or equate one belief system as superior, Granddaughter Crow theorizes and extrapolates an entirely new way for us to understand the great questions of human life. She breaks down the human life span into four distinct stages: awakening, enlightenment, being, and becoming. You'll learn not only where you are now, but how to best navigate your life so that what you become (the energy of the night) is a more pleasant experience.

Follow along as Granddaughter Crow uses her spider medicine to weave a connective web with so many concepts and acts as a bridge between many different cultures, belief systems, and spiritual perspectives. She shares many beautiful personal stories that you'll almost certainly identify with.

The result of Granddaughter Crow's forays into the great wilderness of human belief?

Unity. Balance. Harmony. And most of all, integration.

We owe a debt of gratitude to Granddaughter Crow for her efforts at distilling such voluminous wisdom from varied cultural perspectives, and for affirming that what unites us is far greater than what separates us.

—**Michael R. Smith, PhD**
Founder of Empath Connection
June 2021

INTRODUCTION

We are about to embark on a journey together, so I'd like to give you a little insight into who I am. *Ya'at'eeh*! (That means hello in Navajo.) I am Granddaughter Crow, also known as Dr. Joy Gray. The traditional way to introduce myself in Navajo is to tell you what clan I am born "to" (mother's clan) and what clan I am born "for" (father's clan). I am born to the Biligaana clan and born for the Tachii'nii clan. In short, another Navajo would recognize that my mother is Caucasian, and my father is full-blood Navajo. With that being said, I am a bridge between two cultures. As such, I have found that respecting each culture and its traditions is very important. Hence, when I am referencing something from my Navajo culture, I will let you know.

When I was born, it was said by the elders that I was "born with a calling." Being "born with a calling" is a way to say that an individual has a special gift that will assist others in a positive way. I have always thought differently than my peers. Not only did I feel different than most, but others often pointed it out

5

to me. I have unique approaches to the world around me, and I've enjoyed studying esoteric wisdom as long as I can remember. Concepts within the spiritual realm have always made sense to me—more sense than social norms.

In this book, I will be sharing perspectives on world religions and belief systems. I will also speak about the natural world and how we can relate to it, and in doing so, I will talk about Mother Earth. We all come from Mother Earth. My belief is that, regardless of background, Mother Earth is exactly that—our mother. I was born into and raised under the Christian faith. I was raised to be a reverend of that faith, but then I started considering other ways of perceiving the world around me. I was around fifteen or sixteen years old when I began to question my belief system. This was considered blasphemous by my family and their religious convictions, and I went out into the world by myself at the age of seventeen. Because I questioned the Christian faith, I was asked to depart from my family.

I gave birth to my son when I was twenty years old. As I was raising my son, studying world religions was one of my hobbies. As my son became more and more independent, I found myself with some free time, and I began my college career at the age of thirty. During my undergraduate studies I took a world religions class—I loved it. I was seeing the world from so many different perspectives, yet I found so many similar conclusions. In my adult life, I found myself returning to a world *before* the Christian church; I studied a variety of cultures and belief systems, and I learned about the approaches that humankind has taken in order to explain how we got here, where "here" is, and what is to come.

Yes, I love mythology, psychology, sociology, and philosophy. Each of these I have studied on my own.

I began to consider that as individuals, we move about our day and about our life based on what we believe. If you believe that you will go to a heaven or a hell based on your actions, you choose your actions in suit. However, if you do not believe that there is a heaven or a hell, you base your decisions, actions, and ethics on something else, like self-worth. I am not suggesting that one is correct and one is incorrect; I am simply making the point that what we believe in dictates our actions.

I moved through college and achieved two undergraduate degrees in business. I continued my education and received an MBA, and I have my doctorate in Leadership and Organizational Development. While I pursued these degrees, I continued to study my other interests on the side. In 2008, I opened Major Consulting, LLC, doing business as Granddaughter Crow. I am also internationally recognized as a Medicine Woman and come from a long lineage of spiritual leaders and esoteric wisdom.

So … maybe I was born with a "calling" after all. And that calling cannot be defined by a certain religion or belief system. Maybe each of us finds our own calling; we simply need to define what it is and what we wish to do with it. I believe my mission in this lifetime is to inspire, encourage, and empower individuals to be their authentic self. I imagine a world where this would be the norm, and it feels like heaven to me. Thank you for being a part of my heaven, for if you weren't open-minded like me, you would not be reading the words on this page.

Within the pages of this book, we will be considering the over-arching topics of awakening, enlightenment, being, becoming, and what is beyond life on Earth. Each chapter is dedicated to one of these topics. These are very broad topics, yet they flow in and out of our daily lives, the four bodies of existence, the natural world, a variety of religions, science, the tarot, and our lifetimes. We are going to explore these topics from each of these positions. At the end of each chapter, I have provided exercises and journal prompts for you to engage in deep self-reflection. My hope is that these exercises and prompts allow you to tap into your inner wisdom. I believe that your greatest teacher lies within you, as that is where wisdom solidifies itself.

Before we begin, I would like to provide you with more insight on how we will be exploring each of these topics.

Concepts in My Life

In each of the chapters, I share a personal story that relates to that chapter's concept. My hope is that by sharing my story, I will inspire you to consider your own story. Everyone has a story; it is based on our experiences and our impressions of those experiences. One might say that my story is about a curious individual who never stopped learning about herself and the world around her. I would say that my story is about courage in the face of fear, self-love in the face of ostracization, and joy in the face of life lessons. I'd like to start my story from the beginning.

When I was a little girl, I was brought up to believe one way. I was told that this way was the only way, and that no other way was the right way—dogma. As a teenager, I began to ask questions, as most teenagers do. Not simple questions, but hard questions. Like, *If the path that I am walking says god loves all, yet some never learn of this god and this path and those people go to hell, how is that a loving god? Why was I created by a creator and given a mind that is curious in nature, yet I am not allowed to use it? To that point, why was I given a mind at all if I am supposed to blindly follow? Why are we so afraid of questioning something or someone?*

I was told that to question was a sign of irreverence and a position of rebellion. Hence, if I questioned but believed blindly, all was well; however, if I questioned and then examined concepts, I had sinned. This was confusing to me. I thought, *I am told that I have free will, but I am supposed to blindly believe in something or someone without choosing that for myself?* The answer—at least in my community—was yes…we were given free will, but we should choose this path blindly, and by doing so, we would show our love to this deity. That sounded manipulative to me. It felt like someone was saying, "I will give you a choice. But you have to choose the one that I want you to choose in order to be accepted." That didn't seem fair to me, and yet, there are many belief systems that have this subtext to them.

To me, it felt like I was being controlled by an unforgiving dictator, a person that supposedly knew everything, and I was supposed to trust them blindly. Sorry, not my cup of tea. So, I continued to ask questions, even though I was raised under the strict doctrine that I should *not* question authority, I should *not* question god—*I should not question.* I argued, "Why do I have a curious mind if I am not allowed to use it?" This questioning continued until I found myself on my own in this world, outside of this indoctrinated system.

I left by biological family days after I graduated from high school at the age of seventeen. To this day, my biological family will not speak to me except in an attempt to save my soul from a hell that their beliefs taught them I will go to because I parted from their beliefs. I find it utterly amazing that their belief system caused them to reject me, yet they tell me that it was my choice/fault because I don't believe what they believe. My life may be an extreme version of this type of thinking, but this mindset is more common than you might think. It extends beyond religious beliefs; this way of thinking can be applied to race, sexual orientation, gender—to just about everything. I was committed to moving beyond this limited mind frame.

As I stepped into a world that was very different from the one that I was raised in, I began to observe that I had freedom, a right to choose, a right to speak, a right to *be*. This was what I desired all along! I approached my new world with awe and curiosity. Yes, I was seen as naive at that time by my peers; I suppose that I was. But that was okay—I was up for the adventure.

I still remember my first day of college. I was attending a class established for new students to introduce them to higher education—General Education 101. My professor was a nice older woman with a kind, inquiring voice. In order to get to know one another, she asked the class, "If you were to write a book, what would the title be?" We took a few minutes to think about our answers and write down the name of our book. As we went around the room and shared, I started to get the sense that I misunderstood the assignment. One person said, "The name of my book is *How to Ski*." Another individual mentioned something about baking good desserts. *Uh oh*... When it was my turn to share, I knew it was too late to change my answer, so I said, *"Belief, Being, and Beyond!"*

The room went silent, and heads tilted as glossy eyes looked at me. In an inquiring tone, my professor asked me to share more. I opened up and took a leap of faith. I explained that I noticed that whatever a person believes—even if it is the simplest belief—constitutes how they behave in the world. For example, if you believe that your teeth will fall out if you don't brush them twice a day, I bet you will brush your teeth religiously. Then I said, "But what if there is something *beyond* what we believe and how we are behaving in the world?"

I left that classroom with a sense of wonder. I knew that my still waters ran deep, so to speak. Decades later, I still haven't stopped asking questions, seeking answers, or learning. And now here I am, writing the book that was born within me oh so long ago.

Concepts in the Four Bodies

There is a school of thought that we have four bodies of existence: the physical body, the emotional body, the mental body, and the spiritual body. These four bodies combined make up an individual. Although there may be more bodies of existence, we will work with this model of the four bodies as a starting point.

The Physical Body

The physical body is tangible and solid, like the earth. It holds a physical age—a certain physical maturity. The physical body is a part of nature (earth) just like a tree; it is strong, balanced, and in a continuous state of self-healing and rebalancing.

The physical body needs nourishment, rest, and exercise to remain healthy and fit. The physical body receives nourishment through the food we feed it. Exercising to keep the physical body fit and strong requires exertion. In order to rest the physical body, we relax and sleep.

The Emotional Body

While our physical bodies correspond to the strength of the earth, our emotional bodies are fluid. Emotions move like water. They can be refreshing as they ebb and flow. They can come in waves, moving through you and, at times, overtaking you. Or they can be stagnant, lacking movement, and you can sink into a depressed state.

The emotional body has an emotional age; however, the emotional age is not necessarily in direct correlation to the physical age. Emotionally, I can feel four years old in one moment and forty years old in another, depending on what I am emotionally encountering. Have you ever encountered an individual who is fifty years old physically, yet they emotionally respond as a five-year-old in certain situations? Moreover, have you ever encountered a ten-year-old who holds the maturity of an elder?

The emotional body needs nourishment, rest, and exercise to remain healthy and fit. The best nourishment we can give our emotional body is positive emotion, such as understanding, love, grace, peace, and joy, to name a few. Exercising our emotional body can be accomplished by keeping an open heart and connecting with the world around us. The emotional body needs rest (downtime) in order to maintain health. Emotional rest can be found in moments of peace and calm.

The Mental Body

The physical body corresponds to the earth. The emotional body flows like water. The mental body behaves much like the air. Thoughts flow in and out. At times they can be as random as a breeze. They can spin like the spiral of a funnel cloud, up and out, or spiral into themselves like the eye of a hurricane. They can be calm and gentle.

According to Alfred Binet, who published the first intelligence test in the early 1900s, the mental body has an age.[1] Binet's test was adopted a few years later by Louis Terman, a psychologist at Stanford University, and this resulted in the IQ test that we know today.[2] The revised system measures a person's intelligence quotient with a percentile system that uses 100 points as the average score. Yet, mental age—like the ebbs and flows of the air—can change depending on an individual and situation. When an individual is tired, hungry, stressed, or simply not feeling well, it will impact their mental age. Hence, the mental body's age can move backward and forward in its maturity.

It is worth mentioning that mental intelligence is not the only type of intelligence we have. In 1983, Howard Gardner introduced the theory of multiple intelligences. This theory suggests that traditional psychometric views of intelligence are too limited; different types of intelligence can be housed in the mental body, physical body, emotional body, and spiritual body. Howard Gardner outlines his theory and suggests that, to date, there are nine different types of intellect:

---

1. Benjamin, "The Birth of American Intelligence Testing."
2. Benjamin, "The Birth of American Intelligence Testing."

- Naturalist intelligence ("nature smart")

- Musical intelligence ("music smart")

- Logical-mathematical intelligence ("number/reasoning smart")

- Interpersonal intelligence ("people smart")

- Bodily-kinesthetic intelligence ("body smart")

- Linguistic intelligence ("word smart")

- Intra-personal intelligence ("self smart")

- Spatial intelligence ("picture smart")

- Existential intelligence ("life smart")[3]

Regardless of how many types of intelligence there are, the mental body needs nourishment, rest, and exercise to remain healthy and fit. The mental body loves food for thought. Consider an idea that you haven't had before; this not only feeds the mind, but it exercises it as well. An individual does not need to adopt every thought that travels through their mind; some thoughts simply need to be recognized and released. It takes a strong mind to entertain a thought that it does not adopt. The ability to hold a thought and focus on that thought takes a healthy mind.

The Spiritual Body

The spiritual body is inspirational; it is like fire. It can keep us energized and inspired. The age of a spiritual body can fluctuate and expand past the physical, emotional, and mental bodies, hence the saying, "That person is an old soul." I have found that

---

3. Gardner, *Multiple Intelligences*, 9–21.

when an individual begins their spiritual path, they may do so for one of two very different reasons: one reason is to grow and develop; the other reason is to escape from reality.

Like a newborn, when the spiritual body is awakened, it benefits from being nurtured and watched over by another. However, after a while, the spiritual body will have to learn how to take care of itself. As the spiritual body develops more and more, an individual has more and more responsibility to attend to themselves and to the world around them. If an individual is on the spiritual path in order to escape from reality, the individual usually abandons said path once they are required to assume spiritual responsibility. There are many spiritual paths. One thing that most spiritual paths have in common? The spirit must be nourished.

▲ ▼ ▲

As discussed, the physical body aligns with the element of earth, the emotional body relates to the water element, the mental body connects to the element of air, and the spiritual body relates to the element of fire. These four basic elements create everything that we perceive within the natural world. We will be exploring the four bodies in more detail in the coming chapters. However, in short, the four bodies correlate with the process of manifestation. First comes an idea, which takes place in the mental realm. Next, we act on this idea with a spirited nature. As we begin to take action, we shift our emotions to match the direction we are headed, and we adjust and readjust our emotions as needed. Finally, through this process, what once was an idea becomes manifest in the physical realm.

Concepts in the Natural World

The natural world flows through cycles. Some cycles take just a day to move through. Others take a season to complete and these seasonal cycles will make up a full year. Larger cycles take a whole lifetime to complete. In each chapter's section on the natural world, we will be examining how that chapter's overarching theme is expressed within the natural world. The chapter themes flow as such: awakening, enlightening, being, becoming, and what is beyond all of this.

The daily model of morning, noon, evening, and night holds wisdom and insight that we can apply to our lives. The yearly cycle of spring, summer, autumn, and winter is an even bigger cycle with similar messages for us. And the cycle of our very own life— from birth to adolescence to adulthood to elderhood—reveals a macro model of the micro twenty-four-hour day. Each one of these cycles allows us to dig deeper into the natural patterns of Mother Earth. Additionally, each one of these cycles, once completed, rolls into the beginning of the cycle once again—another day follows a night, another spring follows a winter, etc. As we move throughout this book together, may you personally identify each of these natural world cycles within your personal story. May this provide a deeper connection within your life and the natural world.

Concepts in Religion

What lies beneath our myths, legends, and lore? Why do so many different belief systems all hold some commonalities? Most belief systems have a creation story, a flood story, a savior or hero story, an end-of-times story, and a story of the afterlife. These common elements reveal the human psyche to us in differing myths, legends, and lore.

I am not here to question the accuracy of any belief system; I am here to examine what drives the commonalities between belief systems. So, why do different belief systems have so much in common? I believe the answer to this question is, "Because of the cosmos and the natural world." The word *cosmos* comes from the Greek word *kosmos*, which means order. As humans, we need to spot patterns and place them into an order or system so that we can have a sense of who we are and where we came from. Can we make it through the natural world's cleansing process? Will we be spared? Is there an end? And if so, where do we go?

Simply stated, our varying belief systems may have similar roots. All belief systems come from a need to understand our human experience, the natural world, and the cosmos. Moreover, belief systems based in religion (which is human-made) are merely our interpretation of human experiences. Some individuals, including myself, would say that they are not religious. I am not religious, however, I consider myself to be very spiritual. My personal spirituality is nature-based; however, I do connect with a plethora of Divine deities.

This brings me to another thought process. I believe that the Divine will reveal itself to us in the best way for us to understand what it is. I may relate to the Divine differently at different stages of my life. When I needed a loving shepherd, Jesus appeared. When I needed to get out of a victim role, Lilith appeared. When I needed a model of a strong yet beautiful female, I met Freya. These deities and all the others I have connected with have guided me through many walks of life. Differing ideas and concepts helped me become the best version of myself today, as tomorrow I will be born once again, just like Buddha.

I may relate to a Divine presence differently than someone else. I believe that the Divine is big enough to reveal itself to each of us in a way that we can identify and relate to; it can come in whatever form we need it to. Some would say that the Divine didn't create us in its own image; moreover, we created it in *our* own image in order for us to relate to this unseen order of life. Hence, a lot of times we will place a human feel to the Divine so that we can understand it—a father or mother role, for example. Of course, some subscribe to the idea that life does not have an order at all. However, I would say that the natural world shows us this order and balance through the movement of the sun, as a basic example. Tomorrow the sun will rise in the east and set in the west. There is a larger pattern to everything.

Some individuals will approach the cosmos and place a masculine version of it within their minds; others may approach it with a feminine image, and others will identify it as androgynous. To that I say, "Whatever makes sense to you. For me, it is all and none of the above." What do I mean? I can relate to the masculine/feminine/androgynous version of the Divine in ways that humans define themselves in their relation to the Divine. Hence, if one or all of these assist you in connecting to the Divine, that is wonderful. Or maybe you do not attach the Divine to any of these terms. There might be something more, something that is outside of these generalities. The Divine is everything from the unseen/unknowable, to what we can awaken within ourselves, to the moment of enlightenment, to the application of energy, to the manifestation of that which is now in the natural world. Hence, the natural world is an expression of the personality of the cosmos' "order" of the Universe. The natural world is a manifestation of the Divine, and so are we.

Some may approach the Divine as a deity because they were raised to believe in that deity and never questioned the reason (or were told not to question). Some will approach different deities because of the attributes that said deity holds. For example, Ganesh, a traditional Hindu deity, is the one who removes obstacles. Freya, a Norse goddess, is the goddess of female empowerment and beauty. Changing Woman, a traditional Navajo deity, is Mother Earth and the season she is clothed in. Ares, the Greek god, is the god of war. What are other deities that come to mind, and what attributes do they hold and wish to share with you?

Some may say that the Divine is simply conscious energy, and some don't see it as a real deity but more as an archetype of energy. For example, some may see Ares as a deity, some would say that Ares is simply an energy that holds characteristics of war, and some would say that Ares is a constellation within the heavens or an astrological sign (Aries).

Again, whatever position you take, allow it to make the most sense to you. Life is about how we relate to and connect with the unlimited aspects of the Divine and the cosmos. What ideas do you have? Do you believe that the stories within the Bible really happened, or do you believe that they are metaphors or parables to show us our history and maybe teach us something along the way?

Concepts in Science

The scientific community also holds beliefs. However, these belief systems are rooted in the scientific method and provable facts; hypotheses that can be repeatedly proven will constitute a truth. Science is open to questions and answers—this is what I enjoy about science. It is worth knowing that science can be broken into two distinct groups, or two different scientific fields: hard science and soft science. *Hard science* is proven through quantifiable results, meaning results that can be quantified through a system of numbers, such as biology, chemistry, and geology. *Soft science* is proven through qualifiable results, meaning results that are not quantifiable; however, they measure the quality of the phenomenon. Some examples of this would be psychology, sociology, and anthropology. Both of these methods are open to exploration and discovery as well as questioning and proof. Some would say that science has directed the natural world (the magickal world). I would say that the natural world (the magickal world) will always leave the scientist discovering more.

Additionally, within the scientific sections throughout this book, we will begin to examine how the religious stories of the creation, the flood, saviors/heroes, and the end of times are represented within science. Although religions require an element of faith in the unseen world, I would argue that science does too. Prior to identifying the law of gravity, didn't we simply trust an unseen force to hold us to the earth? Did we even think to question it? We see the effects of the unseen world through the wind blowing in the trees, through the tides rising and falling, through the sun coming up each morning.

So, when I write about the religious sections, I seek to discover how these same concepts appear within the scientific community. I find it fascinating.

Concepts in Tarot

As we are looking at belief systems, I would be remiss if we did not include the tarot. We will be looking at the correlation between the Major Arcana of the tarot and the five stages of development: awakening, enlightenment, being, becoming, and what lies beyond. Although one might think of the tarot as only a form of divination, its roots go deeper than this; I have even heard that the tarot's roots go back farther than we can see within modern history. However, for the sake of this book, I will draw upon the writings of a Kabbalistic sage, Dovid Krafchow, who wrote the book *Kabbalistic Tarot*.

Krafchow tells us that the roots of the tarot come from the earliest Jewish spiritual tradition, and that the most recent version of these cards have been used for over five hundred years, when the Spanish Inquisition forced the Jewish people to change their beliefs to Christianity. Hence, in order to sustain their own beliefs in secret, the tarot was created with signs and symbols that, if studied carefully, would uncover their ancient belief system. However, these origins far predate modern history. Krafchow speculates that the tarot, a creation of secret sacred cards, came about from the captive tribes of Israel in Egypt.[4] Interestingly, the story of the captive tribes of Israel is reflected in the King James Version of the Christian Bible. So the tarot is not only a form of divination; it holds within it the ancient history and pattern of life

---

4. Krafchow, *Kabbalistic Tarot*, Introduction.

itself from a very longstanding belief system. Huh … it sounds like the tarot may predate the Bible itself; it definitely came about prior to the Christian faith. With that being said, I think that this book would not be complete without examining these ancient beliefs as well. Personally, I love to read tarot and am happy to live in a time when it is quite common to own a tarot deck.

In these sections, I would like you to step into the cards with me. Look around from the position of the main character(s) presented in the card. At the end of each chapter, there will be an exercise provided to remind you how to do this if you would like to journal your experience. I will share this exercise with you now so that you can begin thinking about it as you move through the tarot sections, and I will remind you how to do this exercise at the end of each chapter.

How to Step into the Tarot Card(s)

1. Take a look at the card and see what pops out to you. What does that item or person look like to you? What meaning does it hold for you? What do you see? Write this down.

2. Step into the card. Use your imagination to become one of the characters within the card. From that position, what do you see? What do you feel like? Can you identify with this character? If so, how do you identify with this character? Write it down.

3. Feel into your four bodies. Once you have stepped into the card, go a little deeper into the card by noticing the following:

- What does your physical body sense? It is relaxed, tight, cold, warm, etc.? Write it down.

- What does your emotional body feel? It is happy, sad, confused, uplifted, etc.? Write it down.

- What does your mental body pick up on? Wonder or enlightenment? Or do you hear any words? Write it down.

- What does your spiritual body experience? Does it feel empowered, trapped, a sense of purpose, etc.? If it is difficult for you to extract what your spiritual body is experiencing, I recommend that you take a look at what you wrote down for the other bodies and extract the overarching theme.

4. Journal all these things and you will not only learn more about the tarot cards, but you will also learn about yourself.

If you would like a quick reference guide to see all of the tarot cards together, you can find this in appendix A of this book.

Concepts in Life

At the beginning of each chapter, I share a personal story on the topic of each chapter—awakening, enlightenment, being, becoming, and what is beyond all of this. At the end of each chapter, I extrapolate the overarching topic within each chapter and encourage you to see how these concepts are experienced within your life. My hope here is that you will discover that your life rolls in natural cycles and that there is an overarching pattern to all of us (both individually and collectively). I hope your life makes more sense to you after you read these sections.

We will look at the each chapter's topics through a variety of different lenses. We look at these broad topics through the lenses of the four bodies of existence, the natural world, religion, science, and tarot. Finally, as I described above, I extract the overarching concepts of each of these chapters and show how they can be applied to life. This is the section where we discuss how this happens. It is in this section where you can begin to see how you can create a life that you authentically live.

Journal Prompts for Concepts

I highly encourage journaling. Journaling can be self-reflective and therapeutic, and it can assist you as you mine your inner diamonds—here is how. Have you ever woken up from a dream and felt as though it had a deeper meaning, or that there was a message in that dream for you? You can think about that dream all day long, but you may not be able to extract what it was telling you. Then let's say that you return home after a busy day with the dream still floating around in your mind, so you decide to share this dream with someone: a friend, a partner, a loved one, or your journal. As you begin expressing the dream in your own words, whether that is out loud or in written language, the dream somehow becomes obvious in its interpretation, and it solidifies within you.

Even if this has not happened to you, it is an example of how we can assimilate information through the act of sharing it with another. Journals fulfill this role, allowing you a safe space to reflect without judgment. It is within the act of reflective thinking and sharing that we can identify and integrate the world around us.

In this section within each chapter, I will be providing you with journal prompts. Once you finish a chapter, you can contemplate how those patterns are appearing in your story and in your life. Think of journal time as "me time." Journaling is your time to allow your truths, your thoughts, and your beliefs to bubble up from within you—and your true self emerges.

▲ ▼ ▲

Now that we have discussed the structure of each of the chapters in this book, I would like to take a look at beliefs before we go any further.

Beliefs

Beliefs drive who we are and how we act and interact with the world. To begin, we need to examine the differences between philosophy, religion, and mythology.

Before we move within this delicate topic, I would like to define the terms *ideology* and *theology*. I define the term *ideology* as a system of ideas and/or ideals; ideology is the basis of ideas and how they can shape our worldview. I define the term *theology* as a study of or a positioning of our relationship to a Divine presence, deity, or god/goddess. Basically, how we think and how we relate to something beyond the human psyche or supernatural.

Philosophy

Let's start with philosophy. The entomology of the word *philosophy* takes us back to root words from Greek, Latin, and French.

Philosophy is basically the love of knowledge or the pursuit of wisdom. It is first based in the human experience, but that is not to say that it is without a deity or a form of the Divine. However, one could hold a philosophic basis without recognizing the cosmos or the supernatural. Philosophy can exist on its own with the study of the human experience and the world around us.

The idea or ideology of philosophy can be seen as the study and development of beliefs based on the mind, or the positioning of the mind, in any given situation. It is a very broad word, but my point is that it can exist without cosmic and/or supernatural elements—hence, without a theological basis.

Religion

Now let's explore the term *religion*. This is a touchy word for those who have been harmed or ostracized by a belief that includes a cosmic or Divine influence. Whereas philosophy can be without a Divine influence, religion is based within a Divine presence. There are a variety of ideologies within different religious groups. However, each religion will hold a strong ideology of their own, whether the ideology is that we are all sinners and that we need a Divine presence to save us from ourselves, or that we are here temporarily and our true home is beyond this lifetime.

I am not suggesting that I do or do not believe in different forms of these ideas; however, I am simply stating that these are not necessarily organic concepts. These are ideas that have been taught to us by a system outside of ourselves. I believe that religions are a human-made interpretation of our relationship with a Divine source. Each religion will contain its own theological position. I encourage everyone to research these theological positions prior to blindly following a religious path. Do their ideologies and theologies align with your own? If so, great! Embrace it. My point is that we are free to make our own choices, and again, you should be allowed to question things.

At this point, I do want to acknowledge that many of us are born into a belief system—the belief system of our family. As we grow within this belief system, we should be encouraged to ask questions about it. There comes a time within our lives that we become responsible for what we believe, and for any actions we've taken based on the belief system. I understand that at times, a child will believe whatever it is told; the innocence is pure. However, I also would like to suggest that as you grow within any belief system, you have the right to question it without shame. If it is truly the right belief system for you, it will hold up to the questions.

Not all religions will ostracize a person who leaves the religion; however, there is a subtext in some belief systems that suggests that if you are out of this religion, you are not following the correct path. Now we are getting into more of a cultlike type of thinking. So, at this point, let's move on to the next type of belief: mythology.

Mythology

Let's examine the term *mythology*. I would feel remiss at this point if I didn't reference work inspired by Joseph Campbell:

> Myth goes beyond science and religion, striking the flint-stone of the magical experience at the heart of all things. In a mysterious cosmos, myth is the attempt to explain the unexplainable through the mystical,

leaving us with a sense of astonishment that keeps us engaged and desiring to know more.[5]

When we speak about mythology, we can clearly see that it is full of stories that come to us from beyond ourselves, perhaps from the cosmos. Myths have a mystical edge in order to help us understand that some things are unexplainable, no matter how hard humans try to explain things. In Greek mythology, the twelve Olympians help us understand the attributes of different cosmic and supernatural forces. Within the Egyptian mythological stories, we have Osiris, Isis, Horus, and Thoth. Additionally, Odin, Thor, Frey, and Freya are some popular deities within Norse mythology.

Each of the above-mentioned mythological positionings hold remarkably similar ideology. The purpose of mythology is to assist humans in understanding the world around them and all of the situations and stories that can take place in life. Mythology provides people with a deity that they can call upon and/or worship in their daily activities and throughout their lifetimes. Some deities help with farming, or with travel, or with protection, or with childbirth, or with death. People can work with different deities to gain the support of the supernatural and the cosmos in order to live a full life. I would say that the theology of each of these mythologies holds a polytheistic view and a deep cultural/community expression that links the people with their ancestors.

---

5. McGee, "Joseph Campbell's Four Basic Functions of Mythology."

Compare and Contrast

Now let's take a moment to compare and contrast these three main concepts (philosophy, religion, and mythology) that hold some of the most basic positions for our individual and collective beliefs. The following table is a launching point for us. It is not complete, yet it does help us find similarities and differences in these three concepts.

	Philosophy	Religion	Mythology
Ideology	Study the world around you	Explain the world around you with the help of a Divine source. Additionally, there is a need to be saved by the Divine	Express the world around you with a Divine source that links you to the natural world and ancestors. Not the idea of a savior/hero, but a source that assists you in your life
Theology	Does not require a Divine presence outside of humanity	The Divine is necessary and will vary, depending on the religion	Usually, the Divine is seen from a polytheistic view and as a deep cultural/community expression that links the people with their ancestors

Again, I recognize that this is a basic starting point. However, working from these definitions will assist you in your understanding of this book.

Additionally, there is another aspect that I would like to examine with you. Philosophy can exist without a Divine source, but it may adopt one if the philosopher so chooses. Yet, both religious and mythological positions will inevitably have a Divine source and create various philosophical positions within their belief systems. Hence, philosophy—being the study and understanding of the human experience—is the broadest and most flexible of these three belief systems.

I am not here to ask you to subscribe to one belief system. I am asking you to examine where you are in order to know thyself. I am hoping that you have found a belief system that makes the world make sense, and that helps you make sense of yourself and how you relate to others. Maybe it is the mere fact of believing that helps us make sense of this thing called life. I invite you to question and to examine what you believe. To examine our belief is wise. If you would like more guidance for how to reflect on what you believe, the journal prompt sections at the end of each chapter may benefit you.

I do not see a problem with differing belief systems and worldviews; I find them to be intriguing. I *do* see a problem with a belief system or worldview that is so closed-minded that it judges and undermines that which is different. The beliefs that I hold can be challenged and questioned—I think they should be. A good challenge will either solidify my beliefs or it will dislodge a faulty belief so something more organic can grow in its place.

The concept of closed-mindedness and/or open-mindedness doesn't only apply to certain religions. I have seen so many wonderful people be ostracized or belittled because of the color of their skin, their sexual orientation, or their gender. This type of closed-mindedness can be downright dangerous for individuals and for marginalized groups.

So, what do I mean when I speak about open- versus closed-mindedness? I have observed that an open-minded individual will approach life and situations with curiosity. Open-minded individuals are comfortable with knowing that they do not know everything. They are willing to learn something new or to explore other approaches to things. They willingly entertain an idea or a thought that they are not familiar with. Also, because they have an inquisitive mind, an open-minded person will ask questions in order to understand more about the world around them.

I have personally witnessed closed-minded individuals. I have found that closed-mindedness can spur from an indoctrinated worldview. I have experienced closed-minded individuals who believe that they know more than anyone else—arrogance. They are individuals who are quick to judge when approached with a thought outside of the norm. They will not allow others to ask questions.

I recognize that this topic hits home for me—I am passionate about it. I also recognize that a closed-minded position can be a very comfortable place; if you are closed-minded, your beliefs cannot be challenged and you are not forced to learn beyond what was taught to you. I am not trying to shame anyone here—I understand that at times, and under certain lifestyles, it is very safe to be in a place of indoctrination and strict rules. This indoctrination can create a more predictable life, a more controlled experience, and a safe haven for some. However, this controlled environment can also create a harmful separation from others, even family members.

So, am I saying that an open-minded individual should believe everything they hear? Absolutely not. It takes a very strong mind to entertain a thought that is not adopted. The key is to explore other thoughts and decide which ones you understand, which ones seem fair to you, and which ones do not—you get to choose.

Overview

Now that we have discussed some basics, I want to provide a brief overview of what each chapter of this book will cover.

In chapter 1, we will investigate the unique attributes of the concept of awakening. What does awakening look like from a variety of positions? The mental realm and the element of air align directly with awakening or having an idea. All that we do begins with an idea. The morning, or daybreak, is the awakening of the day. The springtime is the burgeoning of the earth as the year awakens. When we are born is the awakening to life, as is our childhood. We'll discuss a variety of religious beliefs around the creation stories—mankind's awakening.

In chapter 2, we will examine the concept of enlightenment on a micro and macro scale as we think about human existence. The spiritual realm, which aligns with the element of fire, fits nicely into the category of enlightenment. Fire transforms things; it takes something from one state into another through purification and cleansing. The flood stories are about purification and cleansing, as well. Although the flood was working with water, the outcome of purification, transformation, and cleansing aligns nicely. *Spiritual* and/or *spirited* can be defined as passion and action, which is adolescence. The summertime and noon are times when everything comes into the light. This also happens as we become young adults, as we are more responsible and care about how we are being perceived within the community. We become enlightened to how the world works.

In chapter 3, we will contemplate the idea of being. The emotional realm and the element of water hold many similarities to the responsibilities of adulthood and the care that goes into family and career. Additionally, we move into the "real world" during the period of being. This is reflected in the sayings, "Big fish in a little pond" and "Little fish in a big pond." This period of life is a time to consider our goals and to pursue what we consider to be right; we become an example of the savior/hero. We are learning how to be and live in this world. This time of life even touches on the act of baptism; how do you hold and sustain your life when the waves are tossing you to and fro? Many times within our adult life, we reflect on how we got to where we are when it comes to our finances, family, health, etc. These times of reflection are much like the evening time, when things are quiet and we are invited to turn inward.

In chapter 4, we will be exploring the concept of becoming. Whatever we have manifested is what we will live off at this point in life: our 401ks, our pension plans, etc. This is in direct correlation with becoming an elder. Becoming takes us from the day of our youth into the night, the winter, when it is time to slow things down and let things go. I am not suggesting that being an elder is all about slowing down; however, I am suggesting that elders know what is important to them in life and what truly matters. There is a sense of inner knowing due to the full cycle of life they have seen and experienced. Not to sound dramatic or devastating, but the truth is that this is the time to consider the end and to figure out what, if anything, is beyond.

In chapter 5, we will be exploring the concept of beyond. In doing so, we will examine what limited thinking can produce and explore the concept of blind spots. This may sound a little mysterious at this point, but I believe it will make sense once we arrive at that point in the book. We will consider what is beyond all of this. What is beyond your day? Your life? Your belief system?

Each chapter will delve into more details about the cycle of awakening, enlightenment, being, becoming, and beyond. So, take a break if you need it, and then let's go for it!

1

AWAKENING
(MORNING)

An awakening is a time of activation after being asleep.
An awakening can be described as waking up and/or activating. An awakening can happen physically, emotionally, mentally, as well as spiritually. We will go more in depth with each of these in a future section. However, it is good to point this out first, as I want to clarify that we are speaking about awakening on multiple levels.

In the morning, when the sun rises over the horizon and the fresh dew can be found on the ground, this is a time to rise for most of us, to stretch and start anew. (I say "for most of us" because I want to recognize and honor the night owls—the individuals who are awake at night and sleep during the day.) This is the time of daybreak and first light. The natural world is stirring, and the birds are singing. The ground begins to warm as the light of the sun touches it. Within the city, streetlights start shutting off and traffic increases as people head into work. So, this is not only a time when the natural world wakes up, but also a time when the majority of the human population begin their day.

Awakening in My Life

I was born on the Navajo Nation reservation. As a child, I was described as playful, adventurous, and curious. I can recall many new and wonderful experiences as I discovered the world around me: the taste of ice cream, the challenges of climbing a tree, playing in the rain. The world was so fresh and new. My dream was to meet every person on this planet and shake their hand.

My ancestors on my Navajo side were Medicine People. I come from a long lineage of spiritual leaders. My grandmother (*shinálí*) was known to be the giver of names. She held me as a baby and named me "Tranquil Warrior" or "One Who Wars in a Tranquil Way"—this is my spiritual name that my grandmother gave me a few days after I was born. It was said from birth that I would carry on the spiritual aspects of my lineage. My grandfather (*shichii*) had passed years before I was born, but his spirit was seen within me—the spirit of the raven, the spirit of the crow. People who have the spirit of the raven and the crow are individuals who learn within the natural world, who engage in magickal practices, and who fly into the unknown to shed light on situations.

My childhood had some uncomfortable experiences as well. I was born in 1970, and at that time, it was uncommon to be biracial. I had a sense of being different than my peers. If I was with my young Navajo peers, they would say that I was a light-skinned individual, which made me feel like I didn't truly belong. When my family moved to Denver, Colorado, I was surrounded by Caucasian peers, and they pointed out that I looked different than they did. It was an odd time as I was waking up to the idea that I was different.

My ancestors on my Dutch side were indoctrinated Christians, Christian Reformed. With these two influences in my life, it was difficult to gauge my identity as a child. I simply followed the most dominant ancestor's belief system. Have you ever heard the term *spirit filled*? It is based in Christianity; however, it is very liberal for that generation. That was an important part of my upbringing; the practice of "the nine gifts of the spirit" were with me daily.

Here are the nine gifts of the spirit:

1. Words of Wisdom: to provide insight to perplex situations

2. Words of Knowledge: connecting with the Divine consciousness, knowing things that you wouldn't know otherwise

3. Discerning of Spirits: the ability to detect spirits and understand that spirit's message or motive

4. Prophesy: the ability to see the future or foretell future events

5. Speaking in Tongues: to speak in an otherworldly language (a.k.a. heavenly language)

6. Interpretation of Tongues: the ability to interpret otherworldly languages

7. Gift of Faith: the ability to believe in the Divine

8. Gift of Healing: the ability to be a healer

9. Gift of Miracles: the ability to perform miracles

In my elementary school years, I attended a private Christian school. My world and worldview were very protected; I did not listen to secular music (music outside of the Christian faith), and I did not watch secular television shows or movies. I lived in a world of miracles, and others said that I would become a great minister as I held and practiced all of the nine gifts, which had been part of my life since I was in the cradle.

During my childhood, I developed my spiritual gifts and sought spiritual wisdom daily. Adults from my church would ask me to pray for them, and they would even ask me what I saw in the spiritual realm for them. When I was twelve years old, I would get on the local bus by myself and go to church as much as I could; I was at home there. The people in my church and within my community would look at me and refer to me as spiritually gifted—a prodigy. This was my life; this was all that I knew. It was a magickal time of all sorts of awakenings—until I began to ask questions. To be continued in chapter 2.

Awakening in the Four Bodies

What does an awakening look like from the four bodies of existence? In this section, I will begin that conversation with you. However, this section is just a jumping-off point; I would like you to think about how you personally experience awakening in the four bodies. There will be a journal prompt at the end of the chapter that can help you with this.

For the physical body, awakening can be different for each of us. When my husband wakes up in the morning or after a nap in the afternoon, he practically leaps up with a burst of energy. It is like he is excited to start a new day. Me, on the other hand...I like to slowly ease into the day with a nice cup of coffee. I am an avid dreamer, so I also take time to consider the dreams I had overnight. Although these are two very different ways of physically waking up, there are similarities too. We open our eyes and begin to consider what we want to accomplish that day. The act of physically waking up can help us to understand what awakening looks like in the other bodies of existence.

For the emotional body, an awakening can feel like a new start. Maybe you fell in love and your emotional body is waking up to all sorts of feelings—feelings of wonder and excitement; a sense of your heart coming back to life after it has been asleep for a while. The heart begins to beat stronger and open up like a fresh flower. Curiosity takes hold as you wonder what comes next. When the emotional body wakes up to a new day and fresh sensations, it's an exciting feeling! Sensations of hope, of freedom, and of pure joy can be experienced, just to name a few.

For the mental body, an awakening could be described as a moment of clarity, a new idea, or a eureka moment. The awakening can happen gradually, or it can come in one single moment. Regardless, the concept is that a light came on within the mind that revealed things that we did not previously consider. This can happen through meditation, additional education, reading a book, or as you take a walk—there are so many ways to awaken the mental body with new thoughts, ideas, and concepts. Mental awakening is the dawning of new awareness.

For the spiritual body, an awakening happens when the spirit finds an awareness and consciousness of something deeper. When this occurs, it causes the other three bodies to readjust in order to follow in suit. At times, we may seek a spiritual awakening;

however, I have observed that these awakenings usually happen when something profound happens in life. Spiritual awakening may be trigger by an unusual event that causes us to seek out answers, deeper answers. The loss of another can also cause us to question what is on the other side of life. Spiritual awakening has its origins in this thought: *There must be something more than this.* It happens when we are searching for a pattern or explanation for our life, our existence, or our worldview.

Some may find a spiritual awakening through religion or a religious practice; some find it in science; some find it via the natural world. I am not here to guide you to this awakening in one way or another, for I respect a variety of worldviews and spiritual paths. However, with that being said, I have studied many religions and have found that awakenings occur in all of them. A broad example of this is the Bible's creation story. In the next part of this chapter, we will look at a handful of creation stories. Each creation story provides us with some sort of idea about how we came to be.

Awakening in the Natural World

No matter where you land on the face of Mother Earth, the sun will rise in the east. This is a universal law, rather than a human-made law. In your mind, what does the east represent? Here are some examples of what the east means to me.

The sun rises in the east, so thoughts of daybreak and first light dance within my mind. The beginning of a new day, a fresh start. The world begins to warm up with the heat from the sun. Morning dew may form with the sunlight—how refreshing to the earth and plant kingdom. In the morning, I listen to the singing of the birds as my husband feeds them in our backyard. I observe the stirring of the natural world as plants, animals, and the ground itself awaken with the first light of the sun.

In many Pagan and shamanistic practices, the east represents the element of air. The element of air correlates to the mind and thought. The east is where all begins because everything begins with an idea; hence, we can look to the east to find inspiration for a new idea. Coincidently, as I am writing the book, I am facing east.

Additionally, the east is aligned with springtime. Just as the sun rises in the east to start a new day, spring is the reawakening of Mother Earth. In springtime, new animals are born and seeds are planted. Springtime is the morning of a new year.

So, east represents the morning of the day, the springtime of the year, and the start of a new life—creation. Welcome the awakening and birth.

Awakening in Religion

The creation stories that we will examine in this section have a direct correlation with the morning, the springtime, and childhood. All of these can be examined through the lens of newness, coming into being, waking up, etc. In this section, we are going to look at the creation story from the perspectives of Christianity, traditional Navajo stories, and the Aboriginal tribes in Australia. I will go into more detail soon, but first, allow me to provide a brief overview of the creation stories we are going to examine:

- For those who practice Christianity, the creation story is outlined in the book of Genesis.

- In Native American tribes, creation stories work with the concept of moving from one world into the next world.

- The Australian Aboriginal people have a creation story that directly correlates with the morning time.

Other examples of the beginning can be found in traditional Hinduism. The beginning is outlined in the *Rig Veda* and the *Brihadaranyaka Upanishad*.[6]

In the beginning, what happened? Well, I suppose that depends on what belief system you have, but all belief systems align with the idea that in the beginning, there was an awakening.

The Christian Creation Story

In the King James Version of the Bible, the creation story goes like this. In the beginning, god created the heavens and the earth. In short, it took six days, and god rested on the seventh day. On the first day, god created light and dark. On the second day, heaven and earth were created. On the third day, plants covered the earth. On the fourth day, the sun, the moon, and the stars were formed. On the fifth day, animals of the sea and land were created. On the sixth day, the earth welcomed Adam and Eve—the first male and the first female. Finally, on the seventh day, god rested.

Some believe that each of these days was literally twenty-four hours apiece; this belief speaks to how awe inspiring and how powerful this god is. Some take the stance that each day represents a thousand years, referencing 2 Peter 3:8, "But, beloved, be not ignorant of this one thing, that one day is with the Lord

---

6. Leeming, *World of Myth*, 29–30.

as a thousand years, and a thousand years as one day." This is also speculated to mean that one twenty-four-hour day on Earth is not the same measurement as god's day. Hence, each of these days could actually correlate with the story of evolution—bridging both Christianity and science. However one chooses to adopt or interpret this creation story, it still seems very straightforward. This is rather a short story compared to the Navajo creation story.

The Navajo Creation Story

In the Navajo Nation, the creation story is passed down from generation to generation, as the Navajo Nation was an oral culture up until one to two hundred years ago. To the Navajo, the story of the beginning is referred to as "the first world." Humans evolve within each new world. Currently, traditional Medicine People say that we are in the world of three dimensions; however, because this was an oral culture, some may say we are in the fourth or fifth world. You may find different information when researching Navajo creation stories; just a heads up.

The Navajo creation story is called *Diné Bahane'*. In this story, there are four worlds, and each world emerges into the next. The first world, also known as the Dark World, was described as a small island in the center of four seas. Each of these four seas had a guardian: Eastern Sea was guarded by Big Water Creature, Southern Sea was guarded by Blue Heron, Western Sea was guarded by Frog, and Northern Sea was guarded by White Thunder. Above each sea was a cloud—black, white, yellow, and blue, respectively. From these clouds, the first woman and the first man were formed. The first woman started a fire, and so did the first man. The light from these fires represents the mind's eye of awakening.

They recognized the fire within each other and came together. Additionally, the island had insects and bat people, also known as the Air Spirit people. There also lived two coyotes, one was called Great Coyote, the other was called First Angry. Well, as legend has it, much conflict broke out. Hence, the First Woman, the First Man, and all the other creatures found an opening in the sky and emerged into the second world.

The second world was also known as the Blue World. This world held blue birds and blue-furred creatures, also known as the Swallow People. The Air People and the Swallow People lived in harmony for twenty-three days until one night, a being from the Air People wanted to approach the wife of the Chief of the Swallow People with less-than-honorable intentions. The Air Spirits had not achieved balance with the land, and the land could not sustain all of these beings, so they all had to move from this world to find the third world. They found an opening in the south and emerged into the third world.

The third world was also known as the Yellow World. In this world, there were two great rivers. The female river flowed from north to south and the male river flowed from east to west. Where these rivers crossed was named the Crossing of the Waters. In this world, there were six great mountains. The mountain in the east was White Shell Mountain. The mountain in the south was Turquoise Mountain. In the west was Abalone Shell Mountain. In the north was Big Sheep Mountain. In the center of all four of these mountains were two other mountains—Banded-Rock Mountain and Great Spruce Mountain.

The Holy People lived within these mountains, and they traveled on the rainbow. The Holy People visited First Man and First

Woman and performed a ritual that transformed them into human form. After a while, First Woman gave birth to many sets of twins. The Holy people took each set of twins and taught them how to live in harmony, and they populated this world. In the center of this world lived Spider-Woman and Spider-Man—they taught First Woman and First Man how to weave. There was some drama between the females and the males and they separated for a while. Once they got back together in harmony, everyone celebrated. Then, for the next few days, animals ran past the camp, running from some type of danger. The humans sent locusts as scouts to see what the animals were running from. It was a flood; there was a great wall of water coming. The humans grew a single reed that reached the sky and climbed up it to emerge into the fourth world.

The fourth world was also known as the White World. This is the world that we are now in. In the beginning, the sun, moon, and stars were created. The sacred mountains reappeared (and they are still surrounding the Navajo Nation). The seasons were created in this world, as well as the months, which each hold a meaning. In this world, time was created; hence, the idea of life and death came. This is the world where we as humans learned how to live in harmony with Mother Earth. It is known that if we do not live in harmony with Mother Earth, we will have to move to another world.

The Aboriginal Creation Story

When looking at world religions and belief systems, there are so many versions of the creation story. The Australia Aboriginal people have a creation story that speaks of a time when everything on earth was asleep—except for the father of all spirits, who was the only one awake. He woke the Sun Mother so that she would wake up the earth. Later, she gave birth to two children, the morning star and the moon. These two gave birth to what are now recognized as our human ancestors. I find this story compelling, as it has a direct correlation to the morning time. The sun wakes up, the morning stars and moon are born, and from them our ancestors are born.

▲ ▼ ▲

These are just a few of the different creation stories out there. Of course, you can believe whatever speaks to you or whatever you identify with. My point is that each way of life has a creation story of some kind—a story of a beginning. A time prior to what is now known. A time of creating the sun and the moon. A time of creating humans. This creation point is much like the dawning of a new day, the first light, a time of waking up—a time of awakening. These stories show us various versions of what the term *awakening* depicts within the world and within a day for us—macro and micro. Similar characteristics are held among all of these stories: waking up, birth, dawn, first light, sunrise, and awakening.

Awakening in Science

From a scientific standpoint, awakening could be tied to the Big Bang Theory, which provides us with an idea of how the Universe was created. There is also the worldview of the evolutionists and the theory of natural selection. It is most widely recognized from Darwin's theory of evolution. Charles Darwin came up with the theory that life began from a primordial soup, so to speak. Only the strongest of the species, meaning the most adaptable and dominant ones, would survive. And at some point, homo sapiens would emerge with an idea of self-awareness and take over the planet.

From the research that I have done thus far, science is still exploring a variety of theories and trying to prove these theories, so this is an ongoing process. Although science does not have a widely agreed-upon understanding of how planets, stars, and life on Earth came into being, this is yet another example of the human race trying to find a creation story.

Awakening in Tarot

The concepts of awakening can be seen within the Major Arcana in the tarot. The creation story directly correlates with the first five cards within the tarot, in my humble opinion. Of course, there are many ways to perceive the tarot. I find this correlation to be intriguing, yet not limiting. Before we dive in, I want to mention that there are numerous tarot decks out there. One deck that is very popular is the Rider-Waite-Smith deck. Throughout this book, I will be referencing a deck based on the design of the Rider-Waite-Smith tarot, as it is widely recognized. If you have another tarot deck that you would like to reference while reading these sections, you might not be able to find many of the mentioned elements, or you may find an artistic version of these elements in other decks as well.

0. The Fool

In the Fool card, we see the principles of beginning something new. The Fool is off on a new adventure. This is the starting point of a fresh journey. In the card we see a young individual whose stance seems to say that he has little or no care in the world. He is cloaked in the black background of a cape, which to me suggests the unknown—we don't know what  we don't know. This is the epitome of a fool. On the cloak we see ten wheels, which I think represent the ten sephiroth on the Tree of Life within the Kabbalah, the ten realms and/or worlds. The inside of the cloak is reddish in color, the color of love and/or passion. His undergarment is white, the color of purity and innocence.

The Fool faces a blue sky with the sun in full array. It appears that he is the anthesis of an adventurous spirit.[7] From a Kabbalistic point of view, the beam of light that falls upon the Fool is that of the Creator taking notice of this type of adventurous spirit.[8] According to Krafchow, the attributes of this card are "beauty and truth" and the keywords are "power of faith."[9] The carefree Fool holds a white flower in his hand, which I think represents the purity of the unfolding that is yet to come. Within his satchel is the symbol of each of the four elements, which will be awakened

---

7. Waite, The *Pictorial Key to the Tarot*, part II.
8. Krafchow, *Kabbalistic Tarot*, chap. 2.
9. Krafchow, *Kabbalistic Tarot*, Tables of Card Associations for Major Arcana.

in the next card, the Magician.[10] As we view this card, we see that the Fool is about to step off a cliff, which can be interpreted as a leap of faith. In the Fool card we also see a loyal companion: the Fool's dog. Maybe the dog is going to jump with the Fool, or maybe the dog is trying to warn the Fool. Either way, the dog is beside the Fool on his journey.

The Fool is ruled by the planet Uranus, a planet of freedom and free-thinking. Uranus rules the astrological sign Aquarius. Aquarius is the sign of the water bearer, the bringer of new consciousness—the awakening.

Other aspects that one can extract from the Fool card are child-like innocence, a free spirit, hope for future endeavors, potential, a starting point, stepping out of a comfort zone, and taking a risk in a new way of life—all aspects of an awakening.

I. The Magician

THE MAGICIAN.

The Magician in this card can also be seen as the alchemist. The Magician stands under a canopy; it symbolizes the ability to bring spirit into flesh. He stands with one hand to the heavens and one hand pointing to the earth—as above so below. This is introducing the heavens to the earth, just like in the creation stories. As the Magician stands before a table, the point of focus, he lays out all four elements: earth, air, fire, and water. These elements were in the Fool's satchel, and now it is time to put them into action. These four elements working

---

10. Krafchow, *Kabbalistic Tarot*, chap. 2.

together are the basis of creation; they create all things within the natural world. Once again, we have a youthful individual, and above his head is a lemniscate—the infinity symbol, meaning everlasting life force. According to Krafchow, the attributes of this card are the same as the Fool card, "beauty and truth," and the keywords are "power of heart wisdom."[11]

The Magician is ruled by the planet Mercury. In Roman mythology, Mercury was the messenger of the gods; when a god spoke, everything was created. The Magician will become a channel of transformational energy, and he brings the cosmic energy into manifestation.[12] This statement, once again, aligns this card with manifestation and creation.

Other aspects that one can extract from the Magician card are changing thought into form, creative control, and mastery.[13] This takes us back to not only the creation stories, but also the overarching theme of this chapter: awakening.

II. The High Priestess

The High Priestess is a female who appears to be an oracle or a psychic. She sits between two pillars. The white pillar signifies masculine attributes on the Tree of Life, and the black pillar signifies feminine attributes on the Tree of Life. One could see these pillars as indicative of Adam and Eve or First Man and First Woman.

THE HIGH PRIESTESS

---

11. Krafchow, *Kabbalistic Tarot*, Tables of Card Associations for Major Arcana.
12. Kenner, *Tarot and Astrology*, chap. 2.
13. RavenWolf, *Solitary Witch*, 341.

The letter B is on one pillar, and J is on the other. B is the second letter of the alphabet, and J is the tenth letter. These two letters together add up to the number twelve, which aligns with the twelve astrological signs and again draws our focus from the earth into the heavens.[14] At the top of these two pillars, I see a lotus flower. I interpret the lotus flower as power and beauty that is continuously unfolding.

In spiritual groups, we often refer to seeing "beyond the veil," or seeing beyond this world into the next. This is how I perceive the High Priestess—she sits positioned between the veils that separate this world from the next. The fabric that we see behind the High Priestess has pictures of pomegranates. When I look close enough, I begin to wonder if the placement of these pomegranates is the same as the placement of the sephiroth on the Tree of Life. Her crown holds the symbol of the three phases of the moon. She is cloaked in a beautiful blue garment; it seems to flow off the card like the beginning of the stream of consciousness that we will see in the cards to come.

In her arms, the High Priestess is holding a scroll with the word TORA showing. This could mean several things. If you rearrange the letters, you could spell Taro. Taro means "Greater Law, the Secret Law."[15] I also wonder if these letters are meant to signify the Torah, which is the Hebrew term for the first five books of the Hebrew Bible. One of those five books is Genesis, which includes the creation story. Speaking of the creation story, the High Priestess resembles the Divine feminine, who resides in the Garden

14. Krafchow, *Kabbalistic Tarot*, chap. 2.
15. Waite, *Pictorial Key to the Tarot*, part II.

of Eden.[16] I find it remarkably interesting that the Garden of Eden was mentioned by another author as I was conducting my research for this book—it supports my theory that the High Priestess card correlates with the concepts of a creation story.

According to Krafchow, from a Kabbalistic point of view, the attribute of this card is "understanding" and the keyword is "listening."[17] Interesting that the keyword for this card is listening, because the Magician card is ruled by Mercury, and Mercury was the name of the messenger of the gods. It stands to reason that someone needs to be on the receiving end of that message.

I see the High Priestess as an oracle. At times she will share what she sees, and other times she will not speak. This card is ruled by the moon. This is the first Major Arcana card that reveals to us the moon's energy. The moon is the planet of feelings, instincts, and intuition. I see the moon as a luminescent beauty in the night sky. Just as it pulls the ocean's tides, so does it pull the emotions within us. Just as the night sky holds the mystery of the unseen world, so does the moon hold the secrets of the night sky.

Other aspects that one can extract from the High Priestess card are psychic abilities and intuition. This card represents the subconscious mind being explored to reveal the mysteries that lie beyond a very thin veil.

---

16. Waite, *Pictorial Key to the Tarot*, part II.
17. Krafchow, *Kabbalistic Tarot*, Tables of Card Associations for Major Arcana.

III. The Empress

The Empress is depicted as the imperial feminine energy of a pregnant female. She also represents the mother and the feminine energy that gives birth to all. She is the mother of ideas, the feminine who sets into order all that is. She could also depict Eve or the First Woman of the Navajo creation story. I have even heard the Empress compared to Mother Nature herself.

The Empress card is ruled by the planet Venus. This alignment with Venus reveals sensuous energy. This card makes me think of the *Venus de Milo* sculpture too. Venus is also known as the morning star, which takes us back to the creation story from the Aboriginal tribes.

According to *Kabbalistic Tarot*, both the Empress and the Emperor cards represent the right side of the brain. Under this premise, a light comes in through the right side of the brain and is motivated by a question. The light is called *chokhmah*. This Hebrew word refers to the "Power of What."[18] This light within the brain causes us to ask questions in order to gain direction. Hence, our soul is initially driven by asking a question. The spirit entering the physical world sounds like a form of birth, which also speaks to creation.

Within the card, the astrological sign of the planet Venus is in a heart-shaped object to the right of the Empress's throne.

---

18. Krafchow, *Kabbalistic Tarot*, chap. 2.

She wears a crown of stars—twelve stars, to be exact. I believe that these represent the twelve signs of the zodiac.

Other aspects that we can extract from the Empress card are abundance, fertility, motherhood, and the feminine.[19]

IV. The Emperor

THE EMPEROR.

The Emperor is depicted as imperial masculine energy, equal to our Empress; he is the Adam to the Eve, the First Man to the First Woman. The Emperor is the masculine version of manifestation through action.

As we look at this card, we see that the Emperor is cloaked in red—just like the red planet that he represents, Mars. Mars is the ruler of the astrological sign of Aries, the ram. Notice that rams adorn his throne. If you look closely enough at his crown, you will see that the astrological symbol of Aries is on the top. The Emperor is ruled by the astrological sign of Aries, and he has great warrior energy. In Greek mythology, Ares was the god of war. The astrological sign of Aries is ruled by the planet Mars. In Roman mythology, Mars was the god of war.

The Emperor holds a scepter to indicate power and authority. The scepter that he holds is in the shape of an ankh, which is an Egyptian symbol of life and/or everlasting life. This, again, gives the Emperor dominion and power over this world. In the background I see mountains—the kind of mountains that rams like to climb.

---

19. RavenWolf, *Solitary Witch*, 341.

Reflecting on the concept that we just explored from the *Kabbalistic Tarot* within the Empress card, both the Empress and the Emperor cards have a spirit that can express itself in the physical realm. Both hold the Power of What. The Emperor and the Empress are considered to represent the right side of the brain. They send messages to the left side of the brain to be processed. The Emperor sees what is external and obvious, whereas the Empress sees what is internal and/or hidden.[20]

Aspects that we can draw from this card are the masculine forms of leadership, authority with male attributes, and power. However, if you look closely at his eyes, the Emperor is looking back at the Empress card to double-check his decisions.

▲ ▼ ▲

To wrap up this section on the tarot and how it expresses the awakening:

- The Fool represents a new world and new adventures.
- The Magician is bringing heaven to manifestation on earth.
- The High Priestess is a form of the Garden of Eden.
- The Empress represents the First Woman.
- The Emperor represents the First Man.

Again, this is simply another way to explore these concepts. I hope that you are finding this as interesting as I am.

---

20. Krafchow, *Kabbalistic Tarot*, chap. 2.

Awakening in Life

At the beginning of this chapter, I provided personal examples of my awakening by sharing stories from my childhood. In this section, I will be sharing an example of personally identifying with the concepts of the morning time. I will also discuss my personal springtime, my personal creation story, and my personal awakening. Through all of these experiences, one concept holds true: beginning.

The Question

How do we begin a conversation, a dialogue? Conversations begin with an introduction—who I am and what I would like to say. Next, in order to engage with another to find out who they are and what they would like to speak about, we must ask a question. A simple question can open up a world of ideas. A whole conversation can begin with a question.

Awakening begins with a question. With any good examination practice, one must ask some questions in order to fully understand the situation. An answer can only be as clear as the question. In order to recognize an answer, a question must be posed. If a question is not posed, the answer will still exist; however, we will not recognize it as such. Still, many of us were told not to ask questions. "Do not question authority" was a common saying as I was growing up. *Authority* was deemed to be anyone who was older, parents and/or guardians, teachers, leaders, the church, and god.

But asking questions is a crucial part of learning and growing. When I was in the market to purchase my first home, I received some sound advice from a few sources. This advice was simple to understand, yet it made a huge difference in the way that I went about the process of one of the largest purchases of my life: "Ask as many questions as you wish. Don't ever be afraid to ask any question." That was all the encouragement I needed. I wrote down all of my questions and posed them to my realtor, who was such a kind individual. My realtor loved teaching a young buyer how to move through the process. Some of the questions that I asked even made the realtor question the process of the company that he worked for. At the end of the process, he told me that because of me, he had decided to join a more ethical company. Wow! Asking questions really works.

I regularly remind others of the importance of asking questions. For example, when my son started a new job, he asked me for any advice to make his transition easier. I told him that it was okay to learn by asking questions. I assured him that his new employer would rather he ask a question than make an assumption and waste time and resources. Then I explained a great way to ask a question when you are learning the process of a new organization: when you encounter a problem, stop and think of at least two ways potential solutions to the problem. Decide which solution feels like the best option. Then approach your boss with the problem, a couple of solutions, and your recommendation. This allows your boss to become your teacher and not your problem solver. It also shows your boss that you are open to their direction. Perhaps your boss will provide you with an alternate solution, and this way you are able to learn their process.

My son found relief in that process. He told me that he thought he needed to impress his boss by having all of the answers. I smiled and said, "There are many different approaches to a situation.

Most employers would like to teach a fresh mind rather than someone who cannot adapt to their process." Maybe one of your solutions will get your boss thinking too! Approach life with curiosity and ask questions; it is the only way to gain answers.

Journal Prompts for Awakening

In this section, I will provide you with prompts so that you can consider how you experience the world around you. I invite you to record your responses to these prompts in a journal. You could even use these prompts to start a conversation with others!

1) When you think of the word *awakening*, what comes to your mind?

2) How do you experience awakening? That is to say, what does awakening look like to you within each of your four bodies of existence?

   - Physical body

   - Emotional body

   - Mental body

   - Spiritual body

3) In the section Awakening in the Natural World, we discussed how an awakening is like the morning, springtime, and birth. This is simply a jumping-off point for you to think about what morning, springtime, and birth mean to you. Take a moment and personalize it. How would you describe morning? How would you describe springtime? How would you describe birth?

Take a moment and brainstorm descriptions of what the morning brings. If you find yourself stuck, I have started a list, but I encourage you to take some time and contemplate what the morning means to you personally.

- As the sun slowly rises in the east, I begin to see this first light flow through my curtains and gently kiss my face like a loving mother, welcoming me to a new day.

- As I gently wake up to the bird's song outside my window, I stretch and feel the fresh air and listen to the happy songs of nature.

- The rising sun casts red, orange, and yellow hues across the sky. The rising sun provides a few beautiful moments of the artistic expression of the natural world.

Writing these depictions helps the morning feel more alive. Take a few moments to think about or write down what you experience upon the first light in the morning. There is almost a poetic vibe to this experience. Once you have written a few sentences describing the morning, look at what you have written and change the word *morning* to *awakening*. How does that affect what you wrote?

4) In the section Awakening in Tarot, we discussed a few tarot cards. Now, you can step into the cards and personalize each of them: the Fool, the

Magician, the High Priestess, the Empress, and the Emperor. Here is how to do this:

- Take a look at each card individually and write down what pops out to you. What does that item or person look like to you? What meaning does it hold for you? What do you see? Write this down.

- Step into the card. Use your imagination to become one of the characters within the card. From that position, what do you see? What do you feel like? Can you identify with this character? If so, how do you identify with this character? Write it down.

- Feel into your four bodies. Once you have stepped into the card, go a little deeper into the card by noticing the following:

  ◦ What does your physical body sense? Is it relaxed, tight, cold, or warm?

  ◦ What does your emotional body feel? Is it happy, sad, confused, or uplifted?

  ◦ What does your mental body pick up on? Does it feel wonder or enlightenment, or do you hear any words?

  ◦ What does your spiritual body experience? Does it feel empowered or trapped, or does it feel a sense of purpose? If it is difficult for you to extract what your spiritual body is experiencing, I recommend looking at what you wrote down for the other bodies and extract the overarching theme.

5) After completing prompts one through four, extract the overarching concepts. At this point, you can write a story, a poem, or even a few sentences to assist you in personalizing what awakening means to you.

2
ENLIGHTENMENT
(NOON)

Noon is the brightest time of the day, when the sun is at its highest point in the sky. This is the time of day when it is harder to find a shadow; technically, when the sun is up we are always casting a shadow, and depending on the season and placement of the sun within the sky, a shadow can be found. But for all intents and purposes, the concept of not casting a shadow or finding a shadow is part of the sensation of enlightenment. Our shadow is absorbed by our light, so to speak. This is the time of day when everything seems to be out in the open—nothing is hidden.

The sun shines the brightest when the earth aligns with the light. Its light brings clarity to the lay of the land. The experience of enlightenment also brings clarity, insight, and wisdom. There are many different paths that lead an individual to enlightenment. I have found that enlightenment can come in flashes, and it can also come through experiences, when we realign both with ourselves and with the world around us. There are so many definitions of the word *enlightenment*. When I studied this word and different experiences of being in the state of enlightenment, I found that enlightenment is much like the concept of love—it is difficult to describe, yet when you are feeling it, you just *know*. From a Buddhist point of view, reaching enlightenment is when you find the truth about life and are no longer wondering and searching—nirvana. Some say that enlightenment or being enlightened is to be well-informed; think of the phrase "Please enlighten me." This means "Please show me more," which flows right in line with the concept of noontime.

For me, enlightenment comes in moments. It continues to expand my awareness of the larger questions in life. Enlightenment is the moment that I understand myself, my purpose, and the role that I have in life. Additionally, I find enlightenment when the bigger picture comes into view; it is that moment when I have an understanding of the whole, of the all. But enlightenment is fleeting. I get distracted or tired and I lose sight. Have you ever had a dream only to wake up and realize you can't remember the details? It's maddening! Similarly, moments of enlightenment can slip away. The more that I learn, the more I understand that I don't know very much of anything. This, too, is a form of enlightenment: knowing that you don't know. We may each experience enlightenment in different ways, but it can all be considered one form of enlightenment or another.

Enlightenment in My Life

In the last chapter, we talked about my childhood—from birth until age twelve. This was the morning time of my life. In my teenage years, from thirteen years old to twenty years old, enlightenment came to me. It was wonderful and difficult all at the same time. It was wonderful because I discovered more and gained answers to some of my questions. However, it was difficult because with enlightenment comes a clarity of what you may or may not need to leave behind. Enlightenment encourages you to leave behind old ideas and old concepts so that there is room to grow into a new, more knowledgeable version of yourself.

When I was twelve years old, I moved from a private Christian school to a public school. This was a culture shock for me. I went from a Christian-based school of thirty children per grade to a public school with over three hundred children per grade. (In my Christian-based school, there were about three hundred K–12 students in the whole school!) I was overwhelmed. I carried my Christian Bible to school with me every day, prayed over my lunch before I partook, and dressed conservatively. I was teased because I didn't use bad words and because I was naive to the secular world's music and movies. I struggled every day to understand this different world that I was in. I was constantly overstimulated; I remember convincing myself that I was physically sick so that I would not have to go to school. I don't know how I managed to pass my classes that first year; I think my teachers passed me just to get on with their lives. I missed more school than most.

I struggled to find my footing for a couple of years, up until I turned fifteen. At that age, I began to ask questions about the Christian god. This was seen as the most blasphemous thing to do—especially when the questions were coming from a child who was looked upon as a spiritual prodigy. I fell off the pedestal that I was on, and to say that the church was disappointed in me was an understatement. They believed that the only way this could happen was if I was suddenly possessed by the devil.

They said things like, "Questioning god? Only the devil would question god!" Talk about a fall from grace.

Due to this fall from grace, I was placed back into a private Christian school for my senior year. I must admit that this shift in my life caused suicidal thoughts. At this point, I was failing high school; I didn't care about little things like schoolwork or extracurriculars. I recall asking questions like, "Why did god give us a brain and free will if we have to gain his permission to do the smallest of things and do whatever he says blindly? If god is all about love, grace, mercy, and understanding, then why are you judging me?" Even though I was questioning the Christian faith, I respected it, but the church that I was once a part of asked me to leave. Not all Christian churches do this, but that was my experience.

I spent a lot of time thinking about life and death. Then I was introduced to a new concept: *rebirth*. The answers to the questions I'd been asking started coming from within me in the form of poetry. Here is a poem that I wrote when I was seventeen years old:

> I'm not an empty book
> So you can write the pages.
> I have a pen in my own hand
> That will take me through these stages.
>
> I know you try to make me more,
> But I'm all that I can be.
> I hope someday you understand
> My life is within ME.
>
> Someday you'll look at me again
> And see somebody new.
> You'll see a little more of me,
> And a little less of you.

I recognized that I was struggling with being who someone else wanted me to be instead of being who I truly was. This enlightenment provided me with some answers. I realized that I believed in the form of the Divine that created me to be me. I believed in a form of the Divine that created all types of wonderful and authentic individuals. I believed in myself. With this, I went out into the world in search of this form of the Divine. I also decided to engage with the secular world, a world that I was once told was "bad" or "wrong." I wanted to learn about this new world and experience all that it had to offer.

At the age of twenty, I found out that I was pregnant with my son, Michael. This gave me another form of enlightenment. This pulled me out of feeling lost and gave me the will to live a meaningful life once again.

Enlightenment in the Four Bodies

Just like the sensation of awareness, enlightenment can affect each of the four bodies of existence. This can happen within each individual body of existence, although at times it almost happens simultaneously through each of the bodies. Here is what happens at each individual level and as a collective whole.

When a sense of enlightenment happens on the physical level, it can come in the form of goosebumps and/or chills. There is a sense of something inspiring the physical body's alertness and awareness. There may also be a sensation of feeling lighter within the body, almost as though the burdens that we carried upon our shoulders were lifted so that we actually stand up straighter and taller. Others may even say that the aura of the enlightened individual has changed; think of the glow depicted around saints and deities throughout history.

When enlightenment comes through the emotional body, there is a sense of stillness. I experience a deep sense of peace. Although there can be a sense of excitement and joy within the emotional body, there is usually a sense of calmness too. There can be a sense of emotional openness to the world around you, as though you know that nothing that can harm you emotionally. A sense of confidence may follow. Some may experience emotional enlightenment as a deep level of compassion and connection with the world around them. However it is experienced, emotional enlightenment brings a sense of emotional intelligence with it.

When enlightenment comes through the mental body, there is a sense of clarity. Personally, my mind stops racing and I feel that everything fell into place and makes sense. Mental enlightenment can happen when we hold a question in our mind and finally find the answer to that question—the pieces of the puzzle come together. At times this may be experienced as stillness within the mind, yet other times it is so exciting that the information needs to be shared. However mental enlightenment arrives, it brings a sense of clarity.

What do individuals experience when enlightenment touches the spiritual body? I have found that there is a sense of spiritual lightness, almost like the sensation of floating. Some would say that they have reached nirvana. Others say that they have made it to the next level of their personal unfolding, a deeper level or a higher level. It is the state of feeling purified—much like the story of the flood and how it cleansed the earth. One thing that I have observed is that when the spiritual body touches enlightenment, it flows directly through to the other bodies of existence.

Enlightenment in the Natural World

When we are looking at this section, we are aligning the ideas, commonalities, and similarities between the time of day, the time of year, and the cycle of a lifetime, as well as how they relate to the concept of enlightenment. Also peppered into the section is enlightenment's connection to the four directions.

Earlier in this chapter, we looked at enlightenment's commonalities with noontime. Noontime is the apex of the sun within the sky; it's the time when everything is brought to light. This is the brightest time of the day; many individuals take a break around this time and assess what they have accomplished that morning and what is realistic for them to accomplish that afternoon. Some take the full morning to wake up and start the day, and for those people, noon is the time to begin to take some action, as there is only so much daylight ahead.

When we align the concept of enlightenment with a season, it is easy to see that it aligns with summertime. Summertime has the most hours of daylight and the warmest months. This is the time when the seeds that we planted in the garden grow stronger, taller, wider—things start to develop. Summer is the time when people gather outside for social events. The word *summertime* may make you feel a sense of community or excitement.

Within the life cycle, enlightenment corresponds with developing individuality, which takes place during the teenage years. When I was back in high school, my friends changed noticeably over the summer. In grade school, children play and get along with each other, but by high school cliques have formed, and individuals navigate to one clique or another depending on their attributes, interests, and commonalities. This is the time in life when we become more aware of social systems and how we interact with others.

Now let's take a moment to consider how enlightenment corresponds to the south. In many Pagan and shamanistic practices, the south represents the element of fire. The element of fire correlates to the spirit and action-oriented tasks. This is the time to act on the thoughts and ideas we had in the east. Through mindful action comes insight, knowledge, and wisdom. From insight, knowledge, and wisdom comes enlightenment.

Enlightenment in Religion

In many religions, the flood is the time when everything comes out into the open. Some things must be given up during this cleansing. To me, this is the idea of purification through the sacrifice of old ways and/or ideals. This truly sounds like what happened to me when I was a teenager. I became more aware of the real world and less connected with my parents' ideals. I became more enlightened and less sheltered, so to speak.

In this section, we are going to be examining stories of the flood from several perspectives: Christianity, Navajo, and Hinduism. I will go into more detail soon, but first, allow me to provide a brief overview of the flood stories we are going to examine:

- The story of the flood from the Christian perspective is the story of Noah's Ark.

- There are similar stories within the Navajo Nation where one of the worlds was flooded due to the great water monster.

- There is a flood story in traditional Hinduism when a wonderful savior named Manu arises.[21]

One example of another culture's and religion's flood story can be found in the *Popol Vuh*, the sacred book of the Maya.[22] Within this sacred book lies the story of creation and the flood.

So in religious stories of the great flood, what happened? Well, I suppose that depends on what belief system you have and what side of the globe you live on. Floods happen, and due to their magnitude and potentially devastating nature, they are events that are recorded all around the globe. Even in oral cultures, stories of floods were handed down. Some cultures saw floods as a punishment for the sins of humankind, whereas other cultures—such as the Maya—saw floods as a graceful act of kindness because the floods cleansed and erased mistakes.[23] Others saw floods as a great ending with a new beginning to follow.

The Christian Flood Story

In the Christian Bible, Genesis 8 speaks of a man named Noah. He was known to be a holy man in the eyes of god, even though he lived in a world that had gone wrong. In the King James translation of this text, it is stated that the sons of god mated with the daughters of man and bore children of great strength; it also

21. Leeming, *World of Myth*, 55.
22. Leeming, *World of Myth*, 60–62.
23. Leeming, *World of Myth*, 60–62.

describes giants in the land. (I'll let you speculate on what that means.) Then god looked upon what he had created and said that it must be destroyed. He told Noah to build an ark and said that every creature should come in twos to dwell on this ark with Noah and his family. This would keep them safe during the great flood.

After the ark was built, it rained for forty days and forty nights, and the earth was covered with water. Once the rain stopped, a rainbow appeared in the sky. It was recorded that the rainbow was a sign to Noah that god would never flood the earth again. It was also recorded that the ark had landed high in the mountains of Ararat.

Hence, in this version of the flood story, the flood came to cleanse the earth of its atrocities.

The Navajo Flood Story

First, let's back up to the Navajo creation story that I shared earlier in this book. Remember the third world—the Yellow World where the two rivers flowed and crossed in the middle, and it had six main mountains? This was the world where First Woman and First Man were populating the world, and the Holy People would ride upon the rainbow from the great mountains to teach First Woman and First Man how to live in harmony with each other and the natural world. At that point in the story, all sorts of different animals began to run past the village, so First Woman and First Man sent out locusts to find out what frightened the animals. The locusts returned with news that a great flood was coming—a great wall of water.

Now let's back up. If you recall, before the animals ran past, First Woman and First Man had been separated from each other for a while. The women built one camp and the men built another. Between their camps ran a river. When First Man and First Woman reconciled, they decided to merge camps. When First Man came back to get First Woman and take all of the females across the river, he accidentally left three women behind—a mother and her two daughters. This mother and her daughters were in the field and did not hear the call from First Man. Night was coming and they realized that they had been left behind, so the three women decided to swim across the river to reconnect with the tribe. When they were halfway across, Big Water Creature grabbed the two daughters and took them to her home under the water. The mother made it across the river, reconnected with her tribe, and told them what happened. For three days and three nights, people searched the river for the girls, but they could not find them.

On the morning of the fourth day, two Holy People came to the tribe with a bowl of white shells and another bowl full of blue shells. The bowls were placed in the riverbed and began to spin. The spinning of the bowls opened a portal in the river that led to the home of Big Water Creature. When First Woman and First Man approached the home, they found Big Water Creature asleep, and they also found that she had two children of her own in addition to the daughters she had taken. First Woman and First Man took the human daughters and left the home of Big Water Creature.

That would have been fine and balanced in the eyes of Big Water Creature, as she did steal the girls in the first place. However, the coyote Big Angry decided to cause trouble. Big Angry snuck down the portal and took Big Water Creature's children, unbeknownst to the tribe. The day after the daughters returned home is when the animals started running past the camp. For three days, animals ran past the tribe. On the morning of the fourth day, they sent the locusts to see what was spooking the animals. It was the revenge of Big Water Creature.

In this story, we see that the flood came about from life not being balanced correctly. There was stealing; both Big Water Creature and Big Angry took something that did not rightfully belong to them. Although it was the coyote that caused it and not First Woman and First Man, the flood caused the tribe to ascend into the next world.

Again, I would like to mention that the Navajo people had an oral culture, so these stories may vary within the tribe, and different versions of the worlds can be found. For the purpose of this book, we are simply looking at the idea that the Navajo Nation had a flood story, and this flood came from an imbalance and caused the people to ascend again.

The Hindu Flood Story

Now let's move to the flood story in Hinduism. This story comes from the sacred text *Shatapatha Brahmana*, and it is about Manu.[24] The name Manu is rooted in the Sanskrit word *Manushya*, which translates to *man* in English. The story of Manu has a lot of similarities to the story of Noah.

The story begins with Manu finding an exceedingly small fish that he could hold in the palm of his hand. The fish said to him, "Rear me, and I will save thee."

---

24. Leeming, *World of Myth*, 55.

"Wherefrom wilt thou save me?" Manu asked.

"A flood will carry away all these creatures: from that I will save thee!"

Manu placed this fish in a small jar full of water. Once the fish outgrew that, he upgraded the size of the pool. But the fish began to grow extremely fast and Manu recognized that he couldn't keep the fish, so he released him into the sea, where the fish continued to grow. Manu kept returning to speak with the fish, as the fish was great council. The fish instructed Manu to build a great ship because a flood was coming, so he did. Manu was spared from the flood because he was safe on his great ship. The ship landed on high mountains within India.

I did not find anything in the written text about why the flood occurred; however, maybe it was simply a natural process of releasing the old and welcoming the new.

▲ ▼ ▲

Although there are obvious parallels between the flood stories of Manu and Noah, there are parallels between all three of these stories. Each of these stories showed that we travel from one world into the next, and the flood was an ending that led to a new beginning for the human race—it was a form of ascension.

Enlightenment in Science

"Eureka!" This is a joyful expression when an individual or a scientist discovers something or is enlightened. Enlightenment within the scientific community is the discovery of something new, a formula to create something, or a deeper explanation of the world around us. These are a few examples of what enlightenment looks like within the field of science. Many discoveries were made due to anthropology as well as historic floods.

There are many stories about a great flood occurring, which led me to wonder if there was any scientific evidence that a great flood occurred around the world. J. Harlen Bretz was one of many geologists who nudged the scientific community toward accepting the idea of a massive flood occurrence. Bretz was an American geologist who studied, among other things, caves. His work focused on examining unusual erosion within Washington state. He believed that this unusual erosion occurred due to a great amount of water flooding certain areas a long time ago.[25]

When he first came up with this hypothesis, he presented it to the scientific community and was met with extreme doubt. However, more research was done, and it was determined that Bretz's hypothesis was correct. So science does have records of at least one flood of biblical proportions! I am sure there are many more places around the world where the land will reveal to us that there was a massive flood.

Enlightenment in Tarot

As we've discussed, a variety of belief systems mention a great flood for purification and cleansing. This flood took people from one world to another—they ascended—which led to enlightenment in these stories. In most of these flood stories, a vehicle of transportation assisted those who survived such an event. The flood story correlates with the next five cards within the tarot: the Hierophant is an enlightened priest or authority of sorts; the Lovers replenish the earth like the animals that walked

---

25. Bretz, "The Spokane Flood Beyond the Channeled Scablands," 97–115.

two-by-two from the ark; the Chariot is the vehicle to the next world; the Strength card speaks about courageousness in the midst of overwhelming obstacles (strength during the storm); and, finally, we see the Hermit—the sole being at the beginning of a new world, alone and seeking enlightenment to guide his path and the path of those that will come after him.

V. The Hierophant

THE HIEROPHANT

The Hierophant is the depiction of wisdom through learning and teaching. Here we see the enlightened teacher speaking with members of his community, sharing his knowledge and messages of clarity, insight, and wisdom. He is cloaked in a reddish-orange robe, which is known to be the color of Taurus. And just like the Fool, his undergarments are white, suggesting purity and innocence.

The crown that adorns his head is threefold. I have learned that this represents the threefold nature of life; it is the crown of the universal teacher. The top fold represents the principles of alchemy. In alchemy, salt, sulfur, and mercury are the three principles, and it is believed that all matter can be divided, via alchemical processes, into these three things. The second fold holds the seven chakras within it: root, sacral, solar plexus, heart, throat, third eye, and crown. The third fold represents the five senses: sight, sound, smell, taste, and touch.

Notice the Hierophant's right hand (on the left side of the card). He has two fingers pointing up and two fingers pointing down.

This signing of his hands is called an *ecclesiastical sign*, and it distinguishes between the manifest and concealed parts (or brings into manifestation what was concealed or unseen—the seen and the unseen) of wisdom and knowledge given to us by a teacher or anyone who assists others with the idea of ascension and enlightenment.[26] The keys below the Hierophant's seat represent the hidden knowledge that resides within us; the keys urge us to unlock this knowledge so that we may become enlightened.[27] According to Krafchow, the attribute of this card is "knowing" and the keywords are "intuitive knowing."[28]

The astrological sign that correlates with the Hierophant card is Taurus.[29] Taurus is the fixed earth sign within astrology. Taurus is steady, grounded, and slow-moving, and enlightenment also takes the path of focused and grounded progress; with enough effort, one can sustain enlightenment upon reaching it.

In ancient Greece, hierophants were priests who assisted others through the rites of passage of death and rebirth.[30] So not only does this card represent enlightenment, but it also represents death and rebirth—just like the stories of the flood.

26. Waite, *Pictorial Key to the Tarot*, part II.
27. Krafchow, *Kabbalistic Tarot*, chap. 2.
28. Krafchow, *Kabbalistic Tarot*, Tables of Card Associations for Major Arcana.
29. Kenner, *Tarot and Astrology*, chap. 3.
30. Kenner, *Tarot and Astrology*, chap. 3.

VI. The Lovers

I can easily see how one would relate the Lovers card to the creation story—they resemble Adam and Eve in the Garden of Eden. However, when we examine this card's connection to the great flood, it can represent the animals coming two-by-two into the ark in order to replenish the new world. The Lovers card is about relationships—not only our relationships

with other people, but our relationship with Mother Earth. All is well when we stand together, in balance. This card is also about being naked, i.e., being truthful without hiding. This card can also depict the new world that is ascended into after the flood—enlightenment—as an angel parts the clouds.

In the card, we see the sun is apex in the sky—full light, noontime. The Lovers are blessed as the angel and sun smile upon them. According to Krafchow, the attribute of this card is "foundation" and the keywords are "embracing our nature."[31] Back in a pure world once again.

Astrologically, this card is ruled by the sign of Gemini, the twins.[32] The twins often oppose each other; one looks at one side of an issue and the other twin sees the other side—yet that duality is captured in one sign. This represents the union of opposites; balance and harmony that can be created, even between opposites. How can we reach enlightenment if we are unable

---

31. Krafchow, *Kabbalistic Tarot*, Tables of Card Associations for Major Arcana.
32. Kenner, *Tarot and Astrology*, chap. 3.

to consider both sides of an issue? Gemini is mutable air—intellectual energy. Intellectual energy is needed to gain clarity and insight. Gemini is very curious and always seeking answers; I often say that Geminis learn for the sake of learning.

So we see a fresh start for these two—and the picture of a mountain in the background. Noah's ark ended up on a mountain, and so did Manu's ship, and First Woman and First Man had to climb a mountain to reach enlightenment...

So now where do we go? Let's take a look at the Chariot card to see.

VII. The Chariot

The Chariot is the vehicle we take to move forward in life. The vehicle in Noah's story was an ark. The vehicle in the Navajo story was the reed that grew into the heavens. The vehicle in Manu's story was a ship. The Chariot represents all of these and takes us to our next ascension.

On one side of the Chariot there is a black sphinx. The other side has a white one. This is the same as the Tree of Life—the pillar on one side of the Tree is black (representing feminine energy) and the pillar on the other side is white (representing masculine energy). Another representation of this concept is the yin-yang symbol; one half is black (feminine energy) and the other side is white (masculine energy). This is the same pattern that we noted within the High Priestess card.

The individual in the Chariot represents the self. He stands under a canopy of stars from heaven—working with the heavens, the upper worlds, and the cosmos to drive us toward our next adventure. He is also adorned with a cloak that has the crescent moon on it; maybe he listened to the High Priestess and will carry out his actions with her messages in mind.

According to Krafchow, the attribute of this card is "victory" and the keywords are "external strength."[33] Strength will be covered in the next tarot card, yet this is where it begins—the Chariot is the vehicle that takes us toward our moment of true strength. The Chariot is also deeply tied to the word *drive*. Krafchow writes, "Drive does not come from reason; it has an energy that surpasses even passion."[34] From a Kabbalistic point of view, when we unpack the essence of the word *drive*, we are not talking strictly about the logical mind, nor are we talking about a heart full of passion. Drive tends to be a deeper natural force that is passed down to us from generation to generation in order to keep our species going. Noah, First Woman and First Man, and Manu were driven to sustain the human race; they took their own form of the Chariot to survive the flood. They did this for survival. The deepest form of drive—victory.[35]

Astrologically, the Chariot card aligns with Cancer, which is a cardinal water sign. The summer solstice begins when Cancer is at zero degrees; this marks the first day of summer. Again, this ties into our themes of summertime, noontime, enlightenment, ascension, and the earth's natural cycles.

---

33. Krafchow, *Kabbalistic Tarot*, Tables of Card Associations for Major Arcana.
34. Krafchow, *Kabbalistic Tarot*, chap. 2.
35. Krafchow, *Kabbalistic Tarot*, chap. 2.

Cancer energy is all about the family and the home, and perhaps its tie to the Chariot is a reminder to take a little piece of home on every journey. Perhaps you take your family and two of every animal with you on the ark, or you bring your friends and family with you as you ascend from the third world into the fourth. Home will follow you wherever you go, as home is within the heart. Cancer energy represents family life too; it is interesting that after each of the flood stories, family is found once again.

VIII. Strength

In my studying of the tarot cards aligning with the Kabbalistic Tree of Life, I learned something remarkably interesting: the Strength card lands on the pathway between the pillar of mercy and the pillar of severity. Severity without mercy is cruelty, and mercy without severity is weakness. Hence, the path of Strength must balance between these two concepts. We need to consider when to be more severe and when to be more merciful.

For me, the Strength card signifies that gentleness is not weakness; the woman in the card gently tames the lion and seems to do it with love. Whereas the word *strength* does have connotations to being hard or harsh, this is not always the case. In this card, the lady that tames the beastly lion does so with a balance of severity and mercy. As seen in this card, the yoke (restraint, healthy boundaries) around the lion is that of roses with thorns—it is perfectly balanced as the thorns represent severity and the roses represent mercy.

There is an infinity symbol in this card, placed above the head of the woman, just like in the Magician card—the symbol of everlasting life. This shows us that working our magick is not something that is done in one day; moreover, it takes a lifetime of consideration. Strength is a part of us, yet it can create change that is bigger than us. Strength is learned and earned. We note within this card, once again, the tall mountains in the back and a clear day within the heavens. It takes strength to climb these mountains; it's not for the faint of heart. According to Krafchow, the attribute of this card is "victory" and the keywords are "internal strength."[36]

The Strength card is ruled by the astrological sign of Leo. Leo is ruled by the sun. This chapter is about noontime and the light of day, the time when the sun is at its apex. That certainly weaves in nicely with the concepts of clarity, insight, and wisdom—enlightenment. This card also represents courage and self-discipline. I can certainly see how the individuals who experienced the great flood needed bravery and determination when faced with overwhelming obstacles—Strength in the midst of a storm.

IX. The Hermit

After the flood, the earth became still. Now we come to the Hermit. The Hermit represents wisdom, insight, and illumination. In this card, we see an individual who is standing tall with a glowing lamp in one hand and a staff in the other. Like the Hermit, I light candles to illuminate situations, to bring light into a dim

THE HERMIT

---

36. Krafchow, *Kabbalistic Tarot*, Tables of Card Associations for Major Arcana.

condition, and to bring clarity where it is needed. A staff is something that a traveler would carry to assist them on their climb up a mountain. As we look at the Hermit card, we notice the individual seems to be on a mountain. I wonder if this is how Noah and Manu felt—a little isolated, yet with a sense of arrival. When discussing the Hermit, Waite wrote, "His beacon intimates that 'where I am, you also may be.'"[37] I find this quote remarkably interesting. If I were Noah, First Woman/First Man, Manu, or a flood survivor, I would hold the position of "Because I survived, all children of the earth that are yet to come have survived too." So how isolated is the Hermit, really?

From a Kabbalistic point of view, the Hermit and the High Priestess correspond with the left side of the brain, whereas the Empress and Emperor correspond with the right side of the brain. The right side of the brain is light, and the left side of the brain is dark. A similar effect takes place between what is perceived by the mind (brain) and the masculine and feminine aspects of these two concepts—light and dark; the masculine observes what is obvious, and the feminine perceives what is hidden. So if the Emperor and the Empress are considered to represent the right side of the brain, they send messages to the left side of the brain to be processed. The Emperor sees what is external and obvious whereas the Empress sees what is internal and/or hidden.[38] The left side of the brain is said to be the place where we process information that was sent to us by the right side of the brain. The High Priestess and the Hermit are the counterparts to the

---

37. Waite, *Pictorial Key to the Tarot*, part II.
38. Krafchow, *Kabbalistic Tarot*, chap. 2.

Empress and the Emperor.[39] According to Krafchow, the attribute of this card is "understanding" and the keyword is "hearing."[40]

The Hermit is directly correlated to the astrological sign Virgo. Virgo energy is that of mutable earth—grounded in nature with daily tasks, health, and well-being at the forefront of the mind.

▲ ▼ ▲

To wrap up this section on the tarot and how it expresses enlightenment:

- The Hierophant represents wisdom through learning and teaching—the essence of enlightenment.

- The Lovers represents the purity of relationships and being truthful without hiding, which leads to enlightenment within relationships.

- The Chariot represents moving forward in life on the road to enlightenment. Also, it represents working with the cosmos in order to gain direction and realizing that the balance of feminine and masculine energy leads to greater enlightenment.

- Strength represents that strength is not the absence of gentleness—it is the ability to balance severity and the ego with less ego and more mercy. This balancing act is the strength that one needs on the path to enlightenment.

---

39. Krafchow, *Kabbalistic Tarot*, chap. 2.
40. Krafchow, *Kabbalistic Tarot*, Tables of Card Associations for Major Arcana.

- The Hermit represents the ability to go within and the ability to self-reflect. These are two important aspects that will lead us to enlightenment.

Again, this is simply another way to explore these concepts. Within these cards, we either see enlightenment (the Hierophant and the Hermit) or the road to enlightenment (the Chariot); what it takes to get there (Strength); and that when we come together in a relationship, we can find more enlightenment if we are pure and honest with each other (the Lovers).

Enlightenment in Life

At the beginning of this chapter, I shared some of my personal stories of enlightenment. I shared about the parts of my life that embodied noontime and summertime, as well as the flood of questions and experiences that I survived in order to purify myself. Out of my questions came answers. Most of these answers came from within me—my personal baptism into being authentic. And I learned that the question and the answer both lie within.

The Answer

In chapter 1, we spoke about awakening and asking questions. In this chapter, we will discuss enlightenment and having the answers to any question. The answer can only be as clear as the question. Once we ask a question, the answer magnetically appears—although it may take time and energy to find it. We have to continuously seek the answer. It is much like saying, "When the student is ready, the teacher will appear." I would like to open our minds to the idea that not all teachers are humans. We can ask questions of the natural world, the spiritual world, and the Universe. We can even ask questions of ourselves. I like to say that the greatest teacher lies within you because that is where wisdom solidifies—that is where enlightenment happens.

Here is a fun practice. Years ago, I kept a journal. Well, I had shelves of journals, to be honest. During this time, I noticed a very interesting pattern. In one journal entry, I would pose a question. It was usually an existential question about the world or Universe and why things worked the way they did. I noticed that a few journal entries later, I was answering the question that I had posed earlier. It wasn't on purpose; it simply seemed to happen. At this point, I realized that my questions were alive within me, and part of me was always unconsciously seeking the answer. Even when the question wasn't at the forefront of my mind, I was searching for its answer. This was an interesting phenomenon for me. I realized that questions function as a magnet for the answers to arrive.

Additionally, I have found that sometimes the answer is hidden in the question that we are asking. For example, I was speaking with a young woman a few years back. She asked me, "When will I break up with my current boyfriend?"

I responded, "So you will be breaking up with your boyfriend?"

She said, "I don't know. That is why I am asking you for your insight."

I smiled and told her, "You asked me *when*, not *if*. So, could the answer be that you foresee that your relationship with him will end at some time in the future?"

She blushed and told me that she had been wanting to break up with him, but she wanted an older, wiser person to tell her that it is the right thing to do. I told her to follow her heart. She is happier now.

When an answer comes, it might not always be what we want to hear. However, it is an answer nonetheless. In the next chapter, we will be looking at the idea of taking action on the answers that come.

Journal Prompts for Enlightenment

In this section, I will provide you with prompts so that you can consider how you experience the world around you. I invite you to record your responses to these prompts in a journal. You could even use these prompts to start a conversation with others!

1) When you think of the word *enlightenment*, what comes to your mind?

2) How do you experience enlightenment? That is to say, what does enlightenment look like to you within each of your four bodies of existence?

   - Physical body

   - Emotional body

   - Mental body

   - Spiritual body

3) In the section Enlightenment in the Natural World, we discussed how enlightenment is like noontime, summertime, and the teenage years. This is simply a jumping-off point for you to think about what noontime, summertime, and teenage years mean to you. Take a moment and personalize it. How would you describe each of these?

Take a moment and brainstorm descriptions of what noontime brings. If you find yourself stuck, I have started a list, but I encourage you to take some time and contemplate what noontime means to you personally.

- I recognize that I have had a productive morning and my stomach would like me to refuel my body. I am alive.

- At noontime, my mind is fully awake, yet I am not tired. I find a sense of clarity in the landscape as the sun has ascended to its highest point in the sky. I feel that I am in the brightest period of my day.

- Sitting out in nature as sunlight washes over me, I feel a sense of baptism by light.

Writing these depictions helps noontime feel more alive. Take a few moments to think about or write down what you experience at noontime. There is almost a poetic vibe to this experience. Once you have written a few sentences describing noontime, look at what you have written and change the word *noontime* to *enlightenment*. How does this affect what you wrote?

4) In the section Enlightenment in Tarot, we discussed five tarot cards. Now, you can step into the cards and personalize each of them: the Hierophant, the Lovers, the Chariot, Strength, and the Hermit. Here is how to do this:

- Take a look at each card individually and write down what pops out to you. What does that item or person look like to you? What meaning does it hold for you? What do you see? Write this down.

- Step into the card. Use your imagination to become one of the characters within the card. From that position, what do you see? What do you feel like? Can you identify with this character? If so, how do you identify with this character? Write it down.

- Feel into your four bodies. Once you have stepped into the card, go a little deeper into the card by noticing the following:

   ◦ What does your physical body sense? Is it relaxed, tight, cold, or warm?

   ◦ What does your emotional body feel? Is it happy, sad, confused, or uplifted?

   ◦ What does your mental body pick up on? Does it feel wonder or enlighten-ment, or do you hear any words?

   ◦ What does your spiritual body experience? Does it feel empowered or trapped, or does it feel a sense of purpose? If it is difficult for you to extract what your spiritual body is experiencing, I recommend looking at what you wrote down for the other bodies and extract the overarching theme.

5) In this chapter, we examined answers. How do answers come to you? Do you find answers in meditation? Do you find answers from other individuals? Do you find answers within the natural world? What works for you?

6) After completing prompts one through five, extract the overarching concepts. At this point, you can write a story, a poem, or even a few sentences to assist you in personalizing what enlightenment means to you.

3

BEING
(EVENING)

"To be or not to be, that is the question." [41] Or shall we say, to live or not to live? To be our authentic self, or not to be... This famous statement from Shakespeare's play *Hamlet* is just too juicy not to begin a chapter on being. There are so many levels to being, yet it is simple at the same time: just be. Be the expression of who you truly are without the pressures of limiting yourself to appease another. Just like the word *enlightenment*, the concept of being or beingness can mean different things to different people.

I would say that being is the ability to be present with yourself and the world around you. When you are in a state of being, the mind is calm, not racing with a to-do list. It is a state of recognition of the present. It is experienced from a calm space, when you are relaxed and peaceful. This is much like the evening time, when many of us settle in and begin to relax. A full day has passed, and evening means it is time to unwind. We return home from a good day of work or play. The sun is setting in the west as

---

41. Shakespeare, *Complete Works of William Shakespeare*, 670–72.

we gather for a meal with loved ones, family, or friends. Many of us let down our hair, change into more comfortable clothes, and put our feet up. Evening is a good time to embrace your authentic self, whether you're alone or with loved ones; evening is a time to be completely yourself. This aligns with the concept of being. Again, the experience of being is much like enlightenment, as all of our four bodies of existence relax into the moment. In truth, being cannot be spoken; it can only be experienced.

Krafchow, our Kabbalistic teacher, writes of Moses: "Moses, our teacher, who received the Torah through his attribute of Humility, is often quoted in vexing times as saying *Mah anucnu*, or 'What are we?'" [42] Maybe god was responding to this question by saying, "I am that I am."

When I was being brought up in the Christian faith, I was told that the phrase "I am that I am" was only to be spoken by god himself. But now that I am older and have studied other belief systems, I wonder if god was saying, "Be who you are—be the hero." See, you cannot become a hero until you recognize who you are currently and take responsibility for that. Then you can finally begin the hero's journey, if you so choose.

Being in My Life

What does *being* look like in my personal story? In the previous chapter, we left off at the age of twenty, when I discovered that I was pregnant with my son, Michael. The idea of being a mother gave me hope and clarity. But how was I going to actually *be* a mother? How was I going to be an adult? I had so much to learn.

---

42. Krafchow, *Kabbalistic Tarot*, chap. 2.

A month before my twenty-first birthday—the birthday that some see as the true beginning of adulthood—I had some complications with my pregnancy. I went to the emergency room, and they induced labor. In brief, I will say that it is a miracle that both my son and I survived the birth. I have escaped physical death multiple times during my childhood, adolescence, and adulthood; understanding this aspect of my life can help you understand how broad my life experiences have been. Nevertheless, I was now at the stage of my life when I needed to figure out how to *be* within the world, how to hold and sustain the life that I was given *and* the life that I was taking care of.

At the age of twenty-one, I was a new mother. It's worth noting that I was the youngest of my siblings and didn't even know how to change a diaper. Needless to say, I learned quickly! I didn't have much money and was not married to my son's father. I was in desperate need of financial support for basic necessities, and I qualified to receive government support until both he and I were well and could face the world. This process took a little over two years.

When I was twenty-three years old, I got a job as a receptionist and began to learn the business world. At the age of twenty-four, I became pregnant again. I lost the child. At twenty-five, the same thing happened. Followed by the same situation with my conceived twins at the age of thirty-one. This was a really rough patch of loss for me as a mother, and for my body as a female.

Due to complications from the birth of my first child, I was able to conceive but unable to carry. I decided to have surgery to make sure that I would not be able to conceive again in order to prevent this cycle from happening. Usually, I don't share this part of my life; however, I hope that it helps anyone who is experiencing the same type of situation to know that there is hope in the being and hope in the beyond. Life is not easy, especially when we are going through periods of loss, but it is worth the love that we can all experience and share even throughout loss. At times, loss can wake us up to what we have, who we are, and our beingness.

Between the ages of twenty-one and twenty-five, I grew within my beingness. I learned not to take life for granted. I learned not to take life personally, as well. I learned how to *be* within my life and how to be strong physically, emotionally, mentally, and spiritually. I include this not to elicit a sad response, but to express that *being* is not always easy. In fact, sometimes just being is hard and painful. However, it is taking us somewhere. Being in the moment can be the strongest experience we ever encounter.

I landed a wonderful job when I was twenty-five years old, and by twenty-six I could afford to purchase a home. Some would say it was luck—I believe it was the Divine at work in the background. For a few years I worked my way up the ranks of the corporation, and when I turned thirty years old, I decided to go to college. I recall driving home from work one evening when a thought came to me: *What would I want to do if I could do anything in the world?* My answer? "I would go to college." Remember, I didn't perform very well academically when I was young—more often than not, I thought that I was gifted spiritually, but not mentally. However, I wanted to give college a try.

At the beginning of this book, I wrote about my first night of college. (I attended night classes and worked during the day to pay my bills.) That night I came up with the concept of this book. College passed quickly. I found my inner student and decided to do a dual degree. Years later, I had earned two undergraduate degrees. At that point, I was in my mid-thirties and looking at starting my master's degree. It was about that time that the Divine showed up in my life and pulled me back in. See, after I left home, I tried to ignore all of the spiritual gifts. I believe Great Spirit said, "Okay, go do your thing. But when the time comes, I will invite you back to your calling."

I was thirty-five when I found myself in a metaphysical store looking around. I decided to get a tarot reading, and the reading talked about me rediscovering my spiritual side. The Wheel of Fortune and the World cards came up, and the tarot reader told me that if I rediscovered my spiritual path, a wonderful adventure lay in front of me. It was also around this time that I began to learn about being an empath, and I strongly identified with the concept. Now I understood why it was so difficult for me to make the shift from a small classroom to a large classroom when I was twelve years old. As an empath, there is a tendency to become overstimulated when placed in situations with large crowds of people. I had definitely been overstimulated by the large groups of children, and I was too young to know how to ground and center myself.

After I left the metaphysical store, one experience led to another until I felt empowered enough to nurture my spiritual gifts once again. Same gifts, different belief system. I was finally being myself. I took so many classes on all types of magickal paths. I felt alive! By the age of thirty-seven, I had completed my master's degree and began the adventure of pursuing my doctorate. I was still working my way up the corporate ladder. I loved my home and my son. And I was taking martial arts classes on the side. I had found myself, and life was good. But then my life took another turn.

One night in my martial arts class, I was sparring and I hurt my knee—my ACL tore. I actually heard a popping sound, which meant that it didn't simply tear a little bit, but completely disconnected. When my ACL tore, I fell to the ground. *Now what, Spirit?* I knew that something was wrong, but I didn't know how wrong it would go. It went really wrong, really fast.

I don't recall my torn ACL hurting, and I later learned from a doctor that ACLs don't have nerve endings. However, I was unable to stand on the injured leg without my knee completely buckling, so I went to see my primary care physician, who referred me to a knee surgeon. I learned that, medically speaking, each knee has four ligaments that support the overall function of the knee and leg. The anterior cruciate ligament (also known as the ACL) is the ligament that connects the thigh bone (femur) to the shin bone (tibia). So, when my ACL tore, my leg was not supported, and it would require reconstructive surgery to repair it.

Although the outpatient surgery went well, I contracted a post-operative bleed (a hematoma). What does that look like? Well, I woke up the following morning at home, and my leg was in incredible pain. When I looked at it, it was literally black and blue and all shades of purple, too. Of course, I contacted the surgeon and needed to return to the hospital for a follow-up surgery to repair the bleed and to remove the extra blood. This was an additional outpatient surgery.

If that wasn't bad enough, the medical staff ran some blood tests on me and discovered that I had contracted a staph infection in my blood during surgery. The danger here is that once a staph infection enters the bloodstream, it becomes systemic—the infection was coursing through my entire body. If left untreated, I would have gone into septic shock, which is life threatening. I was on my deathbed and didn't even understand or process that fact.

The staph infection was treated by administering strong antibiotics through an IV (intravenously) three times a day until the infection went away, which took five weeks in my case. Because I needed IV treatment so frequently, they placed a PICC line in me. A PICC line (which stands for peripherally inserted central catheter) is a small tube that was inserted into my inner arm and was threaded up through the vein to my heart. This way, when the IV was connected to my arm, the antibiotics could flow right to my heart and straight into my bloodstream.

I felt like I was in some sort of nightmare that I couldn't wake up from. I remember going to the infectious disease clinic to receive antibiotics and looking around at the other patients, wondering why I was here with all of the people who looked like they were on their deathbed. I still didn't understand what was happening to me.

After five long weeks of having a PICC line in my arm and multiple trips to the infectious disease clinic to either receive treatment or to be given some IV bags so that I could administer the treatment at home, I thought that I was out of the woods. Then my other ACL popped only four months after my first one. This time, I was at a BBQ at a friend's house, and they were asking me about martial arts. After showing off for a few moments, I heard the same pop as before—only in the other leg. I knew the road that lay ahead of me as I had just limped down it a few months ago. I had to have another surgery and take more time off work to recover. Thankfully, this time there were no complications with surgery. At this point, I hung up my black belt and decided to slow my life down a little bit.

All in all, I was bedridden for about nine months in 2007. As hard as this part of my life was, there was a silver lining. During those nine months that had no distractions, as my job was to lie in bed and heal, I realized that I wasn't happy working in corporate America. I realized my true calling—the calling that I heard when I was a child. I realized what I wanted to do with the rest of my life.

In 2008, after I'd fully recovered from my ACL surgeries, I left the corporate world and opened up my own business, Major Consulting, doing business as Granddaughter Crow. At this point, I felt like me. I felt like I was living the life that I was supposed to. I was *being*. This is what being is all about; it is not always a simple journey. Sometimes you have to find your way back to your own soul—to be who and what you are. Be your authentic self, as only you can be.

During my childhood, I began to ask questions. When I was a teenager, I began to receive answers. As an adult, I applied the answers to my life. I had a wonderful life full of ups and downs, learning as I went. What came next? Well … by the time that I was forty, I had developed into what some would refer to as a young elder. We'll talk about that in chapter 4.

Being in the Four Bodies

When I simply am just being, my physical body relaxes. My emotional body is expressing its essence without the need for protective walls. My mind is not second-guessing itself, nor is it thinking of everything that I don't have. My mind is focused on what is right in front of me. My spiritual body feels free—I am who I am. "I am that I am."

In the book of Exodus in the King James Version of the Bible, there is a particular story about Moses. Moses ascended up Mount Sinai, where god gave him the Ten Commandments. Moses asked god who he should say gave these commandments to him, and god responded, "I am that I am."[43] I am not trying to be irreverent, but I, too, am that I am.

Here is a story that I would like to share with you, a story that I heard a long time ago. There once lived a man that did a social experiment. He decided to walk around and identify and connect with the things and the people around him in a very profound way to see the interconnectedness of us all. As he was going about his day, he saw a homeless person, and he realized that if life circumstances would have taken him in a different direction, he too could have been homeless. So he looked at the homeless person and thought, *I am that*. The next day, he saw a wealthy man on Wall Street and realized that if life had taken him in certain directions or provided him with certain opportunities, he could have been that guy on Wall Street as well. So he thought, *I am that*. Over the course of a year, he began to identify with everyone and every walk of life. And after a year, he said, "I am that I am!"

So, how can we get to this place of beingness? I would recommend resting in a comfortable place and breathing in for a couple of counts. Next, hold your breath for a couple of counts,

---

43. Exodus 3:14 (Authorized King James Version).

then exhale the breath for a couple of counts. This will orient your body, your heart, your mind, and your spirit in the present moment, into the now. How do we get to the sensation of being-ness? By just breathing.

Being and beingness include a state of mindfulness. They require the ability to be in the moment and experience all that it holds. Over the past couple of decades, there has been an increased interest in mindfulness and its benefits. Mindfulness can reduce stress, increase focus and concentration, and positively impact overall health on physical, emotional, mental, and spiritual levels.

If you're new to mindfulness, you can begin with a certain type of meditation called *satipatthana* mindfulness meditation. Satipatthana requires keeping your attention inside. There are many forms of meditation that ask you to empty your mind; this is not that kind of meditation. Mindfulness meditation simply asks an individual to pay attention to what is going on within themselves as they move throughout the day. The concept is to be present within each moment and to train the brain to gently come back to the now. There are so many things within our society that distract us. At times, we are multitasking but getting nothing done; driving fast but getting nowhere. I once heard that the human mind will wander off over 40 percent of the time if untrained to focus. It is not necessarily a bad thing for the mind to wander; however, the mind becomes much stronger if it beholds each and every moment with consciousness—if it is present and mindful.

Emotionally and mentally, mindfulness gives us permission to become aware of how we are feeling and what we are thinking within the moment. The idea is that we learn to approach our inner world with awareness and compassion, releasing any judgments. This can lead us to a deeper connection with our emotions and thoughts. When we do this enough, we will begin to spot patterns in our emotional state and mental process. For example, when I began to pay attention to my emotional and mental states, I recognized that I worried or felt anxious for 10 to 20 percent of my day. Once I noticed this pattern, I began to wonder if I was worrying for the sake of worrying—if worrying was a cycle that I navigated each day simply because my mind was used to experiencing it. I began to double-check whenever I felt worried or anxious by asking myself, *Is there something that is causing this anxiety?* Most of the time, I could not think of anything that was going on in my life that was causing me to worry, so slowly but surely, I began to calm myself when this pattern came up. I didn't worry because there was something to worry about, I worried because I was used to it. This same tendency also showed itself in the ways I experienced love, joy, and even anger. As I became more mindful of my emotional and mental states, I began to respond to the current day's situation, not the old emotional patterns that must have been established in my youth.

The spiritual impact of mindfulness is an individual journey and discovery, meaning that everyone will respond differently to mindfulness. However, I have met many mindful individuals, and they all seem more peaceful. Mindful people notice the beauty of the world that we live in. They tend to be more understanding and compassionate. Be aware of what you are focusing on. I once heard a statement that went something like this: "What you practice grows stronger." I don't want to become a stressed out, bitter old woman—I want to become a curious and wise woman. This spiritual journey is very important to me, so I make an effort to focus on things that spark my curiosity and teach me lessons instead of focusing on things that make me upset. As I continue to be present within my life and allow the natural world to communicate with me in a mindful way, I am being enlightened.

Being in the Natural World

No matter where you land on the face of Mother Earth, the sun will set in the west. Again, this is a concept that is a universal law rather than a human-made law. In your mind, what does the west represent? Here are some of my thoughts about the west and the meaning that it may hold for some individuals.

The sun sets in the west, so let thoughts of the relaxing dusk and the glowing lights of the sunset fill your mind. The end of the day is a time to unwind and kick up our feet. The world begins to cool down as evening settles upon us. As the sun sets, we may find ourselves having a romantic dinner with a partner. We may enjoy a glass of wine or another beverage that suits our taste. We may take time to read a nice book or watch a movie in order to get out of our own heads. This is a time when the hustle and bustle of the day are finished, and we can return to normalcy once again. In the evenings, my husband loves to fill our home with gentle music, which helps me relax. We cook together and share a meal, then we spend time letting the rest of the day gently fall away.

The west aligns with autumn. Just as the sunset represents the end of the day, autumn is the time of harvest and represents the end of the summer. The seeds that we planted in the spring, which grew all summer long, are ready to be picked. The ground prepares to sleep before the winter comes. Autumn is a time of maturity within the natural world.

Within the human life cycle, this is the time of adulthood. We have settled into a career, a home, or maybe even a family. Whatever it is that you have settled into is apparent in your adult life. Maybe you haven't settled into any of these (career, home, or family) but have instead settled into your own unique pattern of how to live your life. Whatever this looks like in your story, there is an overarching theme of settling in, holding, and sustaining.

Let's take a moment to consider the idea of the west. In many Pagan and shamanistic practices, the west represents the element of water. The element of water correlates to the emotional world and our emotional body; this is a time to express our emotions. The evening and adulthood ask us to find normalcy and to return to it; we have enough experience to sit back, digest the day, and enjoy life—to simply be.

Being in Religion

In religious texts, it's common to hear mention of a savior. Who is the savior? Well, I suppose that depends on what belief system you have. I would like to examine what makes a savior a savior— what makes a hero a hero. Let's look at the title of hero by examining Joseph Campbell's work, which was widely influenced by Carl Jung's archetype of the hero. According to Campbell, the archetype of the hero has a few common characteristics within all legends and lore:

1. The departure of the hero from his ordinary life. The hero's journey begins with an ordinary walk in an ordinary world.

2. The initiation of the hero to include trials and tribulation. The hero shows us the process of overcoming insurmountable obstacles.

3. The return of the hero. The hero's objective is to do something amazing that can seem unbelievable and to finally return as a hero.[44]

I would be remiss if I did not reflect on Joseph Campbell's complete work on the hero's journey, established in his book *The Hero with a Thousand Faces*. Campbell studied a plethora of mythological stories from around the world and then drew correlations between what was called the *monomyth*, or the hero's journey. So, what is the hero's journey? Well, it is a cycle of sorts. The story begins and ends in the ordinary world, but for most of the story, the hero ventures out and attempts to complete a quest. The quest has its own special cycle, which is evident in this outline of the hero's journey:

1. The Departure

   - The call to adventure

   - Refusal to the call

   - Supernatural aid

   - The crossing of the first threshold

   - The belly of the whale

---

44. Campbell, *Hero with a Thousand Faces*, 48–209.

2. Initiation

- The road of trials

- The meeting with the goddess

- Woman as the temptress

- Atonement with the father

- Apotheosis

- The ultimate boon

3. Return

- Refusal of the return

- The magic flight

- Rescue from without

- The crossing of the return threshold

- Master of the two worlds

- Freedom to live[45]

▲ ▼ ▲

The hero's journey as outlined by Joseph Campbell is a complete list. With much appreciation for his great work, I, too, have observed that there are many similar themes of this list throughout a variety of religious texts and traditions. With that being said, we will not be able to apply every item on this outline to each of the religious views we're discussing in this section. That would take an additional book to express!

---

45. Campbell, *Hero with a Thousand Faces*, 48–209.

The savior's stories and hero's journeys that we will be reviewing in this section have a direct correlation with the evening time, the autumn time, and adulthood. All of these can be examined through the lens of being present, discovering how to be within our lives (taken from the hero's life experiences), normalizing our lives, etc.

In this section, we are going to look at the hero's story from the perspectives of Christianity, Norse lore, and traditional Navajo stories. I will go into more detail soon, but first, allow me to provide a brief overview of the savior/hero stories we are going to examine:

- In Christianity (monotheistic), the savior story is directly referring to Jesus as the savior.

- In Norse lore (polytheistic), there are many heroes, including men, women, heavenly bodies, and even animals or other creatures. We will be examining one of Odin's heroic stories.

- The traditional Navajo hero stories, like Norse lore, have many heroes. Only some of these heroes are depicted in a human form. Other heroes are animals, seasons, and elements—heroes based in the natural world. For the sake of this book, we will be learning about Changing Woman as a hero.

These are a few examples of the hero's story. I believe that for most religions, the hero shows us how to be in the world, how to be in our life, and how to be with ourselves.

The Christian Hero's Journey

As the story goes, the hero is born to an ordinary family.

> For unto you is born this day in the city of David a Savior, which is Christ the Lord. And this shall be a sign unto you; Ye shall find the babe wrapped in swaddling clothes, lying in a manger...And they came with haste and found Mary, and Joseph, and the babe lying in a manger.[46]

In the Bible, the savior—Jesus—was born into an ordinary family and had a relatively normal upbringing. At the age of twelve, Jesus went to the temple and spoke with all the priests. At this point, he not only sought counsel, he provided counsel. We do not hear much after that until he is in his early thirties. Next, the hero story moves into a series of events. He begins to say things like "I am the way," "Follow me," and "Do as I do."

Then, just like Joseph Campbell outlined, it was time for the hero to face his trials. As part of the approach to his trials, Jesus fasted for forty days and forty nights. He was hungry and disillusioned, so this should have been the hero's weakest point—but he prevailed. Then he was nailed to a wooden cross to absolve the sins of humanity. This was the moment of atonement with the father. As the story goes, as Jesus was hanging on the cross the sky grew dark for three hours. It is explained that this is when god turned his back on his son, as his son took on all of the sins of the world. Jesus said, "Eli, Eli, Lama, Sabachthani," which means "My god, my god, why has thou forsaken me?"[47] The hero experienced physical death as well as emotional and mental death.

---

46. Luke 2:11–14 (AV).
47. Matthew 27:45 (AV).

Some would suggest that he went through a spiritual death at this time too. After three days, it was recorded that Jesus came back from the dead and ascended into heaven. I'd say that makes for a pretty good hero.

The Norse Hero's Journey

Odin, the All-Father within the Norse pantheon, sacrificed himself by hanging upon a tree. He did this to find greater wisdom. The story goes that Odin hung upon the tree for nine nights, during which time he was stabbed with a spear. He was not offered anything to eat or drink for these nine nights either. After nine nights, Odin looked at the ground and began to see runes, and he was released from the tree (possibly releasing himself) and fell to the ground. This suggests that wisdom and esoteric knowledge come after a sacrifice or a difficult period, as is outlined in the hero's journey.

After that experience, Odin began to master the meaning of each of the runes. His story suggests that if you wish to find wisdom, knowledge, and understand all that is, you must take it one step at a time. I am sure there are a variety of interpretations of this story; however, this is how I understood it.

Although Odin and Jesus both hung on a tree, they had vastly different personalities. Each of them represents a different position for those who learn about them. Jesus was the model of a shepherd, watching over his flock (in this case, humans) and keeping them from any danger, teaching them how to *be* through parables, and sacrificing his life for them. Odin, on the other hand, was not a nurturing god who took care of his flock. He was a wanderer, a sage, and a shaman. He did not pity the human race or want to save them—that is not why he was on the tree. He sacrificed himself for deep inner knowledge, which we can learn from his journey.

The Navajo Hero's Journey

Although you may not recognize the names of the "saviors" in traditional Navajo stories, you have already met these deities. From a Navajo perspective, a savior is the rain god/goddess showing up during a drought; it is the sun warming the earth after a cold winter. The idea of a savior is more about the Great Spirit (a.k.a. the Divine), the one who creates all that is within the seen and unseen worlds. The Great Spirit created a direct expression of itself within the natural world and within humanity. It is amazingly simplistic in thought and idea, yet it is profound: the Navajo savior is the natural world.

Before I can introduce the Navajo savior, let's take a step back. In the next few paragraphs, I will give you an example of communicating with the natural world on a deeper level than language. The natural world has so much to teach us, but our culture affects our worldview. What do I mean? Well, the language we speak limits or determines our thought process; hence, our language affects how we view reality and our worldview in general. The correlations between our thoughts and the language that we speak is fascinating. Although there are researchers who will claim that this is not true in all situations, I believe that the language we speak has an impact on the way we think and vice versa. For example, the Inuit language holds many sophisticated and subtle words that distinguish the different types of snow. Hence, their language allows them a deeper understanding of snow.

I am bi-cognitive; I think in two different cultures and languages. Biologically, I am 50 percent Navajo and 50 percent Dutch. I was raised in both cultures. This means that I see things from two very different perspectives. I will give you an example.

If I was standing before a tree and someone asked me to get to know the tree, there are two different ways I would approach this because I speak English and Navajo. The English language speaks in terms of labels or naming things, segregating and separating things to break them down into smaller parts to understand the bigger picture. Hence, from an English language perspective, to get to know the tree I would have to separate and name the parts to know the tree. For example, I might think, *The tree has roots, a trunk, branches, and leaves. This is an oak tree.* This type of thinking is very scientifically based and works well most of the time. However, there is another way of getting to know the tree.

The Navajo language describes things and sees things as part of the whole. Hence, in order to get to know the tree, I would need a connection to the tree. I would stand before the tree and notice the complete organism. Next, I would notice that the leaves of the tree were moving in one gentle direction. Then I would notice that my own hair was moving in the same direction. At this point, I would connect with the tree and recognize that there was something—some sort of unseen force—moving the tree and me in the same motion. This is how I would get to know the tree. I am not suggesting that you think in one way or the other; I am inviting you to consider both and find the balance within. When approaching anything in life, do not forget your own totality—your wholeness.

The natural world can be cold, harsh, and dangerous at times, but the Navajo worldview allowed me to understand that that is simply the way that it is. Maybe I am not getting punished by something greater than I. No matter how hard things are, the sun continues to come up. Spring will follow the winter—warmth, fluidity, and peace will return. This is the cycle that nature reveals to us.

By explaining all of this, I hope you understand how the Navajo worldview affects the idea of a savior and the hero's journey. Now, with all of that being said, I would like to introduce you to one deity of the Navajo Nation: Changing Woman.

You have all met Changing Woman, and she knows you too. She changes her dress four times a year. In the winter, her dress is white like the fallen snow. In the spring, her dress is light green like the fresh grassy fields. In the summer, her dress is deep green like the burgeoning plants. In the autumn, her dress is orange, red, and yellow like the leaves changing on the trees. Her hair is the rain; it flows down and brings beauty. The hairs on her arms are the meadows blowing in the wind. The trees are her hands.

Changing Woman is our mother—Mother Earth. What does she teach us? She teaches us the natural flow of life, death, and rebirth. She teaches how to prepare and remain in balance. You can always call upon her, regardless of what culture you come from, because we all come from her and we all return to her. She teaches us to respect ourselves and those around us. She teaches us that we do not "go" into nature because we *are* nature. She is holy because she is nature, and she tells us that we are nature. That makes us holy!

Changing Woman is a different type of hero. Although she does not die, she does usher in the death of one phase of the natural world as it transitions into the next: summer turns into winter, leaves die during autumn, petals fall from flowers, etc. She assists us with balancing our lives as we reflect upon the natural world. She tells us to dress warmly in the colder months. She recommends that we plant when the earth is ready for the seeds to grow. She shows us that shade is welcoming during the hot summer months. She tells us to reap our harvest and prepare once again for the winter. We respect her because she tells us the truth about the natural world, and in doing so, she reveals to us the truth within our lives. For example, maybe you feel like you are in the winter of your career, your relationship, or your health. Maybe this area of your life feels cold. This is not because you have done something wrong or because you are paying for your sins; it is because winter is winter. Prepare for it, and know that inevitably, the sun will bring you a warmer environment. I believe that people experience more suffering when they refuse to change with Changing Woman. Hence, do not refuse to change when it is time.

These are just a few of the different hero and/or savior stories. I continue to encourage you to believe whatever speaks to you or whatever you identify with. My point is that each way of life has a hero or savior story of some kind—a story of a salvation and/or a victor that leads to our beingness. Moreover, these stories help us see a holy and/or sacred way of life within our personal lives through their examples. These stories show us various versions of what the term *being* depicts on both a macro and micro scale.

Being in Science

So, what does being look like from a scientific point of view? I will provide some thoughts and ideas, but I encourage you to come up with some as well. I suppose that being would be considered something the has come into fruition, something that is in a steady state. I can't help but think about the science of baking. The *awakening* stage would be when you decide to bake a cake and collect all the ingredients. The *enlightenment* stage would be when you are combining and creating something new from the original ingredients. Hence, the *being* would be the cake itself. I understand that this may sound a little elementary; however, it is the clearest way for me to describe this process all together.

From a scientific point of view, who would be a savior? Well, I suppose that the concept of savior would be applied to an invention or discovery of something that makes our lives easier. For example, Benjamin Franklin honed and reintroduced electricity to the world through the famous kite experiment. Additionally, when combined, Thomas Edison's direct current energy and Nikola Tesla's alternating current energy brought us electricity. Now we use electricity to the point that it is difficult to live without it. The other day my electricity went out for an hour. This sounds like a short time. However, if you do not know when it will come back on, you start preparing yourself for the long haul. I couldn't get internet on my computer. I couldn't cook on my electric stove. My air conditioning was off on a hot spring day. I checked the battery on my phone to see how long I had until it ran out of charge. It sounds funny, but this experience reminded me how dependent I have become on electricity.

There are other scientific heroes. Maybe a scientific savior would be someone who brings us a theory that allows us to move into a deeper understanding of the Universe. Albert Einstein and his theories changed the way that science views time, space, and the world—and the Universe for that matter. I would say that he is one example of a hero in the scientific community. He held the three basic characteristics of a hero:

1. The hero's journey begins with an ordinary walk in an ordinary world.

2. The hero shows us the process of overcoming an insurmountable obstacle.

3. The hero's objective is to do something amazing that can seem unbelievable.

I would bet that in just about every walk of life, in every belief system, there is a hero. Even within the entertainment industry, we find many heroes. I wonder if we see this archetype so often and from so many points of view because there is a hero within each of us. Yes, there are many phenomenal heroes within legends and lore. Thank them, but don't forget to be the hero you are looking for in this world.

Being in Tarot

These same concepts of the hero's journey can be seen within the Major Arcana in the tarot. The savior/hero story correlates with the next five cards within the tarot.

X. Wheel of Fortune

The Wheel of Fortune card is the symbol of prosperity, breakthroughs, and cycles of opportunity. Some say that this card represents fate and/or destiny. When we look at the Wheel of Fortune card, the largest element to me is the fact that it is a wheel. A wheel is a cycle of cosmic expression. We also notice the letters ROTA, which is Latin for wheel. These are the

WHEEL of FORTUNE

same letters that appeared on the High Priestess card. However, on the High Priestess card, the letters were rearranged to spell TARO. Maybe the High Priestess foresaw fate or destiny within the wheel? I recognize that there is much esoteric mystery around these letters and the words they form. However, I am not knowledgeable enough about this topic, so I will leave these words and their interpretations up to you, if you would like to go down that road. It is a fun one.

Also within this card are different symbols within each corner. In one corner is a man; another corner has an eagle; in another corner, there is a bull; and in the last corner, there is a lion. These images are directly correlated to the four fixed signs of the zodiac. The man represents fixed air, Aquarius. The eagle represents fixed water, Scorpio. (It is said that when the scorpion has reached maturity, it evolves and transforms into an eagle.) The bull represents fixed earth, Taurus. Finally, the lion represents fixed fire, Leo. This card is a representation of air, water, earth, and fire—the four elements working together in harmony to manifest good things.

The Wheel of Fortune carries the energy of all the cards before it and begins to turn, giving birth to a new, brighter, more successful future—sounds like the work of a hero to me.[48] This card represents a time of good fortune and is ruled by the planet Jupiter, an expansive planet that can bring us success and luck. Jupiter is known to be the largest planet within our solar system and rules the fire sign Sagittarius. I have found that Jupiter and Sagittarius hold a very common energy of expansion, opportunity, and success. Having Jupiter rule this tarot card simply expresses more of the great cosmic gift held within this card. Even if read in reverse, I have found that the wheel will keep on spinning until things turn in your favor once again—just like the hero's journey.

According to Krafchow, the attribute of this card is "speech" and the keywords are "the subtle speech of creator."[49]

XI. Justice

The Justice card can be described as a card of fairness; justice is served and all is right with the world again. Justice after a long cold winter would be the sun coming in and warming the earth—a time of equalization. Some would even use the word *karma*. Balance has returned and we can relax once again—the battle of the day is over, and we can retreat to our homes for the evening.

---

48. Krafchow, *Kabbalistic Tarot*, chap. 2.
49. Krafchow, *Kabbalistic Tarot*, Tables of Card Associations for Major Arcana.

Just as within the High Priestess card, the individual is sitting between two pillars—the balance between two opposites or two differing aspects. However, the High Priestess sits between spiritual principles, whereas the Justice card sits between moral principles.[50] The individual holds the scales of justice and balance in one hand and a sword in the other, depicting acting upon justice. In most tarot decks, the sword represents the element of air, which correlates with thought. (Some tarot decks say that the sword represents fire, which correlates with action. Either way, this adds to the meaning of the Justice card.) Because the sword aligns with the element of air, it is in the realm of the intellectual. Hence, Justice has to do with consideration and balance.

In Egyptian mythology, there is a story about the scales within the underworld. Ma'at was an Egyptian goddess who was tasked with keeping the Universe in order and balanced. Kenner writes, "Ma'at, like Libra, was the embodiment of cosmic order: she was responsible for ensuring that the universe followed a consistent, predictable set of rules."[51] It was said that after death, an individual had to pass through the Hall of Judgment, where Ma'at held a set of scales. On one side of the scale was Ma'at's feather of truth. On the other side was the individual's heart. If the scale balanced, the individual could move into the afterlife. Interestingly enough, if you prefer Greek mythology, you may fancy Ma'at as the Greek goddess Themis—they hold similar attributes.

Justice is about weighing truths, but at times it is also about weighing fallacies. Whether or not one wants to believe that another is lying or has an alternative reality where the fallacy

---

50. Waite, *Pictorial Key to the Tarot*, chap. 2.
51. Kenner, *Tarot and Astrology*, chap. 3.

makes sense is not up to me; I will simply state that scales balance truth and untruth in order to come to a logical determination of what the right action to take is. I find it interesting that the symbol of Justice's scales has found its way into many modern courtrooms.

According to Krafchow, the attribute of this card is "knowing" and the keywords are "logical knowing."[52] I think this is so beautiful. For me, this states that you cannot achieve Justice until all things are considered—until all things are known within the mind.

Astrologically, the Justice card aligns with the sign of Libra—of course, because Libra's symbol is the scales. The sign of Libra is ruled by the planet Venus, yet this card also has an element of taking responsibility, which is influenced by the planet Saturn. But back to Libra energy! Libra energy is the energy of cardinal air—the initiator of thought. How nicely that fits with the Kabbalistic attribute of knowing. It is almost like there is a larger pattern here—something that links our dedicated belief systems.

I would suggest with all of this information aligns with the hero's story. Justice reigns! We return to the ordinary world after crisis and rebalance once again. We enjoy the end of our day-to-day adventures and rest knowing that justice is served. But that's only if things work out for our hero … sometimes the hero is hung!

---

52. Krafchow, *Kabbalistic Tarot*, Tables of Card Associations for Major Arcana.

XII. The Hanged Man

Unfortunately, the Hanged Man card is a natural fit here. In so many stories, we think that the hero is in the clear, only for another crisis to occur. As we look at the Hanged Man card, we see many attributes that hold true to the hero's journey. The Hanged Man represents the state of consciousness required to move beyond the ego to the deeper aspects of the self. It is the state of surrender to the law of reversal. His hands are behind his back, reminding us that in this state, we should not meddle. It is time to surrender—hands-off time. The crossed leg also represents a surrendered position, possibly the surrender of the ego and the breaking of the pattern of standing straight up. The Hanged Man is forced to slow down and cross his legs.

The cross or the gallows behind him are made of wood, just like the tree that some of our heroes hung upon. However, it is interesting to me that there are green leaves on this cross. Could it be that this tree was not chopped down? Moreover, is the tree still alive, representing the Tree of Life? I understand that art can have many interpretations; it speaks differently to each individual. This is what I see when I observe this card. What do you see? How does the card speak to you?

It is also interesting to note that the Hanged Man's heart is elevated above his head. In other words, love above logic, which can introduce us to a state of chaos. Krafchow writes, "[Kabbalistically] *chaos* is what precedes logic and is considered one of the higher realms."[53] As Krafchow explains, logic leads us to a singularity of light without an end, whereas chaos is both the light and the darkness, both the pleasure and the will that connects the infinite with the finite. This reminds me of the story of Odin. When he hung upon a tree, he gained wisdom and knowledge—the sacrifice that leads to higher consciousness is also a part of many heroes' journeys. According to Krafchow, the attribute of this card is "pleasure" and the keyword is "open-mindedness."[54]

As the individual hangs upside down suspended in the air, it almost appears that he is in a trancelike state. This aligns with the planet Neptune, which rules this card. Can you relate to the planet Neptune? Although I have been a student of astrology for nearly three decades, Neptune is an energy that is hard to describe. If you find this to be true as well, then you are truly experiencing the energy of Neptune. Words and phrases that describe the planet Neptune are dreamlike, alternate states of consciousness, illusion, fantasy, mystical, even psychic energy. If you think about it, the planet Neptune is composed mostly of ethereal mist and gasses; Neptune is simply impossible to put your finger on.[55]

In astrology, Neptune rules Pisces, the mutable water sign. I think of this energy as the energy of the ocean. It is beautiful and has a depth that holds great mysteries. Pisces has the element of water, hence the element of this card is water. Water is hard to hold in your hand, let alone to put your finger on.

53. Krafchow, *Kabbalistic Tarot*, chap. 2.
54. Krafchow, *Kabbalistic Tarot*, Tables of Card Associations for Major Arcana.
55. Kenner, *Tarot and Astrology*, chap. 2.

XIII. Death

In most savior stories, the savior sacrifices their life for the world as they are put to the ultimate test. The Death card is also an obvious fit in this chapter. But although a hero may hang upon a tree, they don't die—or if they do die, they return once again. Death is the ultimate ending; moreover, it is a new beginning.

Let's examine the Death card together. A skeleton is depicted here—the essential physical structure of all beings in raw form. We may look different on the surface, but underneath we have the same basic structure. And so it is with the hero—they live among us; they *are* us. The skeleton is riding a horse; the horse serves as the vehicle of movement toward change and transformation. Waite wrote, "The horseman moves slowly, bearing a black banner emblazoned with the Mystic Rose, which signifies life."[56] The flower has five petals on it—I subscribe to the numerological belief that the number five represents change. In this case, Death is the greatest change or transformation. We can look at this card from so many perspectives: physical, emotional, mental, or spiritual, or all of the above in one form or another. Regardless of the perspective, this card should not instill fear. In fact, Death is helping us be present and allows transitional cycles to change us and release old ways that no longer work.

Also on this card, we see a young child and an elder. This shows us the beginning and the end, the birth and the death—the full

---

56. Waite, *Pictorial Key to the Tarot*, part II.

cycle of life. In the Rider-Waite deck, there is also a priest on this card. A priest shows up at both the beginning and the end of one's life in most cultures or religions, first to welcome the young child into the world by a baptism of sorts, and then to bless the soul as it goes beyond this life into the afterlife—whatever you believe that to be. I will be examining the beyond in chapter 5 of this book.

In order to understand life, we must understand that death is part of the cycle. As harsh as the death of something or someone can be, it propels us forward into a new life. This knowledge is also part of the hero's story—impending death, impending change, impending transformation. According to Krafchow, the attribute of this card is "severity" and the keywords are "end of cycle."[57]

The astrological sign that the Death card aligns with is Scorpio. Scorpio energy is fixed water. Remember that the sign of Scorpio is not only a scorpion; it can evolve to the form of an eagle, as seen within the Wheel of Fortune card. There is some consideration when we look at the planet(s) that rule Scorpio. Before we discovered the planet Pluto in the 1930s, Scorpio was said to be ruled by Mars. I like to think it is ruled by both. Mars also rules the sign of Aries, the warrior. So, because of Scorpio's ties to Mars, there is a warrior aspect to this sign.

Although Scorpio is a water sign, I would suggest that it is fiery water—and as such, it is not afraid to face what lies beneath the surface. Pluto holds the energy of focused spiritual power and a deep soul capacity to be brought out and refined. It also

---

57. Krafchow, *Kabbalistic Tarot*, Tables of Card Associations for Major Arcana.

holds the energy of death, rejuvenation, and imminent change. Out of the ashes, the phoenix rises. Just like Scorpio's ability to look into the depths of a situation and not be afraid of darkness, so it is with Death. It may not look pretty, but there is a beauty within it. The ability to release old habits, old patterns, and old situations that no longer serve you is a wonderful feeling; there is a liberty within it.

The Death card represents the conversion or transformation of energy into something else. This is the liberty that the hero faces within their journey—to move through the dark night of the soul, only to be reborn as a wiser vibration of self. When we do this within our lives, we come out of the darkness a stronger, wiser being. Be the hero that understands the release that Death brings; it is the ending of that which is finished and the beginning of that which is to come.

XIV. Temperance

Now we will examine the Temperance card. Temperance holds the concepts of patience, stamina, and endurance. Front and center we find an angel—a heavenly being dressing in a white robe. For me, the white robe represents being cloaked in purity: purity of thought, consciousness, and beingness. On the robe is a triangle, the symbol of the element of fire. This angel is pouring from one cup into another. As one cup is higher than the other, I think the upper cup represents higher consciousness and the lower cup is regular consciousness. This is the same message of the Magician card because one of his hands points up and the other down—as above, so below. Next, we see that the individual has one foot in the stream (I like to call it the stream of consciousness that flows around us) and the other is solid on the ground. According to Krafchow, the attribute of this card is "splendor" and the keyword is "patience."[58]

Within this card is focused movement as the angel mixes liquids within two different cups. This can be seen as the alchemical process of mixing two different things like high and low, earth and water, hot and cold, male and female … the list goes on and on.[59] This is the moment of the process versus the outcome—the journey versus the destination.

The Temperance card is ruled by the astrological sign of Sagittarius. Sagittarius energy is adventurous and explorative. Sagittarius is the one who experiences life for the sake of the experience. The sign Sagittarius is ruled by the planet Jupiter. As you might recall, Jupiter was also assigned to the Wheel of Fortune card. This big, expansive planet brings luck and helps us learn and grow.

For many, the virtue of temperance is one of the key directives to living a good life. Hence, the word *temperance* and all of the attributes held within it are virtues that one would find within a hero or a savior. It is the result of the journey that the hero has been on; it is the evening of the story; it is the being that they have become after the long Journey.

58. Krafchow, *Kabbalistic Tarot*, Tables of Card Associations for Major Arcana.
59. Kenner, *Tarot and Astrology*, chap. 3.

To wrap up this section on the tarot and how it expresses being:

- The Wheel of Fortune represents all of the fixed signs within astrology.

- The Justice card brings with it the idea of order, fairness, and balance within the world.

- The Hanged Man card reveals many things, one of which is being in a static state—the state of being.

- The Death card represents transformation. Moreover, it is the state of transforming. It represents the full cycle of our beingness.

- The Temperance card shows us the state of patience, stamina, and endurance—the steady state of being.

Again, this is simply another way to explore the concept of being. Whether fixed, balanced, static, transformative, or steady, all of these are examples of being.

Being in Life

At the beginning of this chapter, I shared my personal story of being an adult—the time that I describe as holding and sustaining. This is what I observe as the evening of my life, where life began to relax into a pattern and rhythm. This is the time where I grew into my own savior as I forged a place in this world. I asked the question *Who am I?* and the answers began to come. In order to live a successful life, we must respond to the answers that have come to us—we must find a way to apply the answers.

The Application

We asked a question. We received an answer. Now what? Well, now that you have the answer, it is time to take action. What are you going to do with the knowledge that you now have? I know that this may sound a bit simple; however, it doesn't always occur to us to take action on what we have learned.

When I was practicing martial arts, the practice showed me how to balance, how to breathe, how to be present, and how to flow with each situation that I encountered. These are great lessons to apply to everyday living. Did I apply these lessons? Well, I wish I could say that I did. The truth is that I only applied these lessons when I was on the mat in class. I did not apply these lessons and answers to my life. If I would have, it may have saved me a little trouble.

I am going to take us back to the concept laid out in the introduction of this book—the four bodies of existence. Have you ever been in a situation where your physical body was in one place, your emotional body was in another, and your mental body was in a different place altogether? I think that when this happens, our spiritual body takes a backseat, as we are not aligned at this time. Maybe you are at work physically, but emotionally you are with your partner or family, and your mind is thinking about what you may need to pick up at the store on the way home. After a period of time living like this, you will begin to feel out of place. It makes sense, doesn't it?

Many years ago, I compartmentalized. I was a single mom of a teenage boy. I worked full-time in an office downtown. I was going to school at night. And, to top it all off, I was working my way toward receiving my black belt. Sounds like a busy life, right? Yeah. It was so busy that I couldn't even hear what my soul was saying. In order to maintain all of these things, I kept them separate from one another. I didn't bring what I was learning in martial arts about balance and breathing into my day-to-day life. I didn't bring what I was learning in school to the workplace. And, of course, I was an entirely different person at home. I was Momma Joy-Joy, the woman who bought pizza for all of the neighborhood kids. I was becoming so tired as I spread myself thin. One day an idea came to me, and I began to reassemble myself. I began to integrate all of my separate worlds, and I began to become more authentic and whole. I did this because I realized that I am like a Stradivarius.

A Stradivarius is a stringed instrument. It is usually a violin; however, you can find a Stradivarius cello as well. These instruments are one of a kind, authentic, and exquisite. They are some of the world's most expensive instruments. They can not be replicated or duplicated, so these instruments retail for millions of dollars. So, what if the body of the violin was in one place, the string in another, and the bow and tuning pegs were in a completely different place? What kind of music would it play? Well, it wouldn't play any music at all. Although it would have all of the makings to play beautiful music, no sound would emit.

Now, what if you are like a Stradivarius? You are one of a kind, authentic, and exquisite. You are supreme and cannot be duplicated, nor can you be replicated. I believe that each of us is this— no one else can be the vibration and expression of your life like you can. Maybe our physical body is like the body of the violin. Our emotional body is the strings. Our mental body is the tuning pegs, and our spirit is the beautiful bow that brings the music out of us. And so it is. We assemble our four bodies of existence and play the expression of life that each of us is. You are authentic, just like me.

As you look at your Stradivarius self, are all the pieces in the correct alignment? Connect your physical body with your emotional body by being mindful of where you are. Allow the spirit to express itself through each of your bodies of existence and bring your beautiful music to the world. Give your emotions permission to express. Give your mind permission to speak. Give each of your bodies a voice. This will help you feel whole once again. Be your greatness, as only you can be.

I believe that if we give ourselves permission to listen to our four bodies, we gain and grow in consciousness. Know thyself and you will know the Universe. And once you know yourself, think about the answer to the question that you have been asking, and then do something about it! Make changes that will help you live your best life. Apply the lessons you have learned. Be the hero you are looking for.

Journal Prompts for Being

In this section, I will provide you with prompts so that you can consider how you experience the world around you. I invite you to record your responses to these prompts in a journal. You could even use these prompts to start a conversation with others!

1) When you think of the word *being*, what comes to your mind?

2) How do you experience being? That is to say, what does being look like to you within each of your four bodies of existence?

- Physical body

- Emotional body

- Mental body

- Spiritual body

3) Earlier, I spoke about assembling your four bodies of existence to flow together. Let's take a moment to do just that. Make sure to write down what you are experiencing as you go through each of these steps:

- Move into an area that you will not be disturbed. You can either sit or lie down—make yourself comfortable.

- Take a few deep breaths and as you release them, relax a little more.

- Feel into your physical body and give it a voice. What does it desire? Does it want more time off? Does it want to go somewhere in particular? What would make it feel good?

- Feel into your emotional body and give it a voice. What does it desire? Does it want more joy? Does it want more peace? Does it want more excitement? What would make it feel good?

- Feel into your mental body and give it a voice. What does it desire? Is it bored? Does it desire a day off? What would make it feel good?

- Feel into your spiritual body and give it a voice. What does it desire? If you are having any challenges feeling into your spiritual body, look at what your other bodies want and extract the overarching theme.

- Once you write down what each different body is looking for, ask yourself what you can do or stop doing in your life that will allow all of your bodies to receive what they are desiring. It will be interesting to see what comes to you.

4) How can we make the changes that will allow us to live our greatest life? This is where you can hone the previous prompt a little more.

- Ask yourself specific questions. These could be questions like what relationships you desire, what career you enjoy, what you should do next, etc. Whatever you wish! The more specific the question, the more specific the answer. For example: "Should I take the job at XYZ company?" "Should I continue my relationship with John/Jane Doe?" "Should I go take a class about ABC?"

- Next, just as we did in the previous prompt, feel into all four of your bodies and give each of them a voice. Sometimes one or more of your bodies will not agree with the rest. If this happens, ask it why. (What is it about the question that disagrees with that particular body?) This leads to deeper insight about what will make you completely happy. Reframe the initial question (statement) until all of your bodies are in agreement. This practice leads to a happier, more authentic life.

5) In the section Being in the Natural World, we discussed how being is like the evening, autumn, and adult years. This is simply a jumping-off point for you to think about what each of these means to you. Take a moment and personalize it. How would you describe each of these?

Take a moment and brainstorm descriptions of what the evening brings. If you find yourself stuck, I have started a list, but I encourage you to take some time and contemplate what the evening means to you personally.

- As I watch the sun set over the western mountains, the colors and textured clouds within the sky reflect the golds, oranges, and hints of red that make me want to relax.

I am simply enchanted by the peaceful artistic expression of the natural world. I have arrived.

- I did it! All my work is finished, and it is time to reap the rewards of a productive day. I return to my place of origin, maybe a little older, maybe a little wiser, and definitely a little tired.

- In the evening, I unwind and settle into my home once again. All is good. All is done. I can simply be.

Writing these depictions helps the evening feel more alive. Take a few moments to think about or write down what you experience in the evening. There is almost a poetic vibe to this experience. Once you have written a few sentences describing the evening, look at what you have written and change the word *evening* to *being*. How does that affect what you wrote?

6) In the section Being in Tarot, we discussed five tarot cards. Now, you can step into the cards and personalize each of them: the Wheel of Fortune, Justice, the Hanged Man, Death, and Temperance. Here is how to do this:

- Take a look at each card individually and write down what pops out to you. What does that item or person look like to you?

What meaning does it hold for you? What do you see? Write this down.

- Step into the card. Use your imagination to become one of the characters within the card. From that position, what do you see? What do you feel like? Can you identify with this character? If so, how do you identify with this character? Write it down.

- Feel into your four bodies. Once you have stepped into the card, go a little deeper into the card by noticing the following:

    ◦ What does your physical body sense? Is it relaxed, tight, cold, or warm?

    ◦ What does your emotional body feel? Is it happy, sad, confused, or uplifted?

    ◦ What does your mental body pick up on? Does it feel wonder or enlightenment, or do you hear any words?

    ◦ What does your spiritual body experience? Does it feel empowered or trapped, or does it feel a sense of purpose? If it is difficult for you to extract what your spiritual body is experiencing, I recommend looking at what you wrote down for the other bodies and extract the overarching theme.

7) In chapter 1 we discussed asking questions. Chapter 2 was about receiving the answers to these questions. This chapter covered acting on the answers to create change. How do you personally take steps toward application? What steps would you recommend to another individual?

8) Upon completing prompts one through seven, extract the overarching concepts. At this point, you can write a story, a poem, or even a few sentences to assist you in personalizing what being means to you.

4

BECOMING
(NIGHT)

After the sun has gone down, darkness covers the earth, and small glimmers of light can be seen in the sky. Depending on what phase the moon is in, we may be able to see it illuminating the sky as it reflects the fallen sun. You may hear the sounds of crickets chirping or an owl hooting. There is less traffic on the roadways, so the sound of nature can be heard with more ease, depending on where you live. Maybe there is more noise in your house as family members return from work, school, or another obligation.

Generally, though, nighttime is quieter than daytime. All is shadow here. Shadow does not mean good or evil. It simply means that it is more difficult to see, and the landscape becomes a little obscure. Curling up to rest, just as the bear who moves into the cave for the winter, we move from relaxation into full slumber. Many of us settle in for a full night's rest. This is a time to rejuvenate—to become new.

Becoming in My Life

In my forties, I began public speaking about spiritual topics. I remember that at several of the events where I presented, I was given tobacco. The act of giving someone tobacco in many Native American traditions was the act of recognition of an elder within the community. It is also good to note that within many Native American cultures, becoming old is respected. Becoming was an overarching theme in my forties.

In 2014, I founded the Eagle Heart Foundation, a nonprofit 501(c)(3) that promotes keeping the ancestors alive through cultural awareness and direct support to give voice to our collective soul. (In 2022, we will be opening the Eagle Heart Academy to serve this mission.) During this time, I still maintained Major Consulting, doing business as Granddaughter Crow. Additionally, I married my beloved husband, Jeffrey Gray. He is the love of my life. I still lived in the original home that I purchased when I was in my twenties, but it had changed a lot. With Jeffrey living in the house, the yard began to develop into a magickal kingdom, as he is amazing with landscaping. Also during this time, I wrote and published my first book, *The Journey of the Soul: The Path of a Medicine Person*.

As active as all of this might sound, it also was a time of slowing down or shifting gears. When I was in my adult years, I was making my way in the world; it was a lot of hard work to hold and sustain all that I was doing. Now, I am a true elder in my ladder years—or a young elder, as the road for me is still long. In this stage of the game, it is time for me to relax and allow, as there is a sense that I have arrived. For me, this means that I am living the life that I was "called" to live since birth.

I look back at the morning of my life, when I felt out of place in the world partly because of the color of my skin; this has completely changed. I was a Native American before being a Native American was cool. I feel blessed that I live in a time where this is changing. I look around at the world from where I stand now, and I see that we as the human race still have so many opportunities to learn and grow.

In hindsight, I can understand my story. See, I am thankful for all of it. If I didn't understand what it was like to experience dogma, ostracization, great loss, being bad in school, being great in school, being in the corporate world, being born, being on my deathbed ... if I didn't experience these things personally, I would not have so much understanding for those around me. I am who I am not despite these things—I am who I am *because* of these things. I have manifested a life that I love to call my own.

Becoming in the Four Bodies

When we rest, we are not only resting our physical body—we are rejuvenating our emotional, mental, and spiritual bodies as well. On a physical level, our breathing slows down. This helps us mentally move into deeper levels of consciousness. We move from beta consciousness, to alpha consciousness, to theta consciousness, to delta. Finally, REM (rapid eye movement) sleep is a place where we can dream. Some say we dream so that our subconscious mind will be able to digest the day's events. As our physical bodies rest, it provides time for our emotional, mental, and spiritual bodies to digest the world around us. Sometimes I experience a dream that provides me with deeper insights from my unconscious mind, which aids my other bodies of existence. When we dream, what is happening?

The scientific studying of dreams is called *oneirology*, and there are a number of different theories around dream state, what occurs, why it occurs, etc. It is hard for the scientific community to come to a firm general consensus on dreaming, as dreams can't be witnessed by anyone but the dreamer. (Unless you have a cool psychic gift that allows you to do so—you never know.) A dream cannot be measured, touched, or weighed in any quantifiable way, but it can be qualified by what is considered a softer research method. However, we do know that sleeping and dreaming help us organize our experiences, and a good night's sleep (which includes REM sleep and dreaming) gives us a clearer mind the following day. Most people don't remember their dreams; however, I have found that if I specifically ask my mind to remember my dreams while I am falling asleep, I tend to remember them.

As a spiritual practitioner, I do find that my spirit can be very active within my dream state. Sometimes my dreams give me messages or are prophetic dreams, and sometimes I have dreams of those who have passed. Although this is exciting when it happens, I have also found that in order to get restful sleep, I ask the other worlds not to visit some nights. Have you experienced this too? My spiritual body loves to astral project and travel around the world. The other night I visited Brazil in dreamtime. Some nights I will be on a planet with two suns and four moons. I enjoy speaking about dreams—but to summarize this, I would simply say that sleeping and dreaming help us solidify our inner world. They are a reprieve after a long day.

Becoming in the Natural World

When looking at this section's natural earth cycles, we are aligning the ideas, commonalities, and similarities between the time of day, the time of year, and the cycle of a lifetime. Also peppered into the section is becoming's alignment with one of four directions.

Earlier in this chapter, we looked at how becoming connects to nighttime. Nighttime is the silent time of the day when we are allowed to shut out the rest of the world and fall asleep to refresh ourselves. We go within.

When thinking about which season becoming and going within are connected to, it is easy to see that this aligns with the wintertime. Wintertime has the shortest days and the longest nights. Winter is also the coldest season. Depending on what region you are in, you may experience snow during this time of year. The sap in some trees moves from the branches to the roots, and these trees become dormant during the winter. This is the time when the ground sleeps. The earth rests so that it has the energy to blossom when springtime arrives once again.

How is this represented in our life cycle? This is the time of the elder. The elder has enough life experience that there is less drive to create a whole new life. This is a time when an individual must get their affairs in order, create a will, and plan for their families to be taken care of after their passing. The realization that they have more time behind them than in front of them may haunt elders; this influences the types of decisions made and the lifestyle lived. Now, don't get me wrong, there are plenty of individuals in their fifties, sixties, seventies, and beyond that still have the energy and drive of a younger person. I am not suggesting that there is a physical age when one must slow down. I am saying that, in general, there comes a time in our lives when sitting on the porch with a nice glass of lemonade makes for the best day ever.

Take a moment to consider the idea of the north. In many Pagan and shamanistic practices, the north represents the element of earth. From earth we have come and to earth we shall return. The element of earth correlates to the physical realm, the realm of manifestation. The phrase "Been there, done that" makes sense here; we are past the point of having to prove something to ourselves or others. This is a time of acceptance and peace. Shore everything up, and we will see what lies beyond.

Becoming in Religion

This takes us to the concept of "the end of times." One could easily correlate this with the nighttime, the time when we fall asleep. Additionally, this relates to wintertime, when Mother Earth falls into a slumber. This is what I am referring to when I share the concept of becoming: the idea that we are headed toward something else based on where we are now. Also, this correlates with being an elder: the slowing down, the depth of wisdom from experience—I hope. The ending of the day, the year, our lifetime…

So what is the end of times, and what does it look like? Well, I suppose that depends on what belief system you have. In this section, we are going to look at the end of times story from the perspectives of Christianity, Norse lore, traditional Hindu legends, and the Navajo story. I will go into more detail soon, but first, allow me to provide an overview of the end of times stories we are going to examine:

- In the Christian Bible, this is depicted in the book of Revelation. There is a concept of Armageddon and the rapture—the end of the world as we currently know it.

- Within Norse legends and lore, the end of times is referred to as Ragnarok—the destruction of the world.

- In traditional Hinduism, the end of times is known as "The End of the Kali Age."[60] However, much like traditional Navajo culture, the ending of one age leads to the beginning of a new age.

- In the Navajo culture, the ending of one time rolls into the beginning of a new time. In Navajo culture, we recognize "the first world," "the second world," etc. Hence, we believe that the end isn't actually the first ending, and it will not be the last—the concept being that the world and our worldview continues to change, and we must honor and adapt to each new world.

Pulitzer Prize winner and *New York Times* columnist Thomas Friedman writes in his book *Thank You for Being Late* that when Mother Nature poses a challenge, she doesn't reward the strongest nor does she reward the smartest. Moreover, she rewards the adaptable—the ones who respect her, the ones who correlate with her, the ones who honor her.[61]

---

60. Leeming, *World of Myth*, 81–82.
61. Friedman, *Thank You for Being Late*, 157–86.

The Christian End of Times Story

First, we will start with an overview of the end times shared in the King James Version of the Christian Bible. Most of this is outlined in the book of Revelation—the last book of this version of the Bible. The book of Revelation is a letter written by a man named John that was sent to seven different churches within the province of Asia, according to Revelation 1:1–4. Seven was seen as a number of completions, based on the seventh day, when god rested in the book of Genesis. If you read Revelation, you will see the number seven come up time and time again. This book is a prophecy; god came to an individual—in this case, John—and shared the story of what was to come in the future. This story begins with the Revelation of Jesus—the returning of the savior. "I am the Alpha and the Omega, the Beginning and the End, says the Lord [Jesus], who is and who was and who is to come, the Almighty."[62]

Within Revelation, there are numerous signs and symbols that can be interpreted in different ways. Hence, as a child growing up in a Christian household, I heard several interpretations of what the end of time would look like. The end of time felt so real and imminent to me that I remember giving this excuse to adults in my life: "I thought that Jesus was going to come overnight, so I didn't think it was productive to do my homework or clean my room." I digress.

In Revelation, John saw a vision of Jesus, the king of the world, standing among seven lights, which was symbolic of the seven churches that he was writing to. John wrote to seven churches

---

62. Revelation 1:8 (AV).

with their own states of affairs. Some of them were behaving in an immoral way, and others who remained faithful were being persecuted. The message was that things were going to get worse—a tribulation was coming. This tribulation was going to ask everyone to choose between unfaithfulness and faithfulness.

At this time in history, the Romans had passed a law that killing the followers of Jesus was legal and acceptable. So, the pressure was on; it raised the question "Are you going to die for Jesus like he did for you?"

Revelation says, "He who has an ear, let him hear what the Spirit says to the churches. To him who overcomes I will give to eat from the tree of life, which is in the midst of the Paradise of God."[63] This section of Revelation promised that if you gave your life for the cause, you would live with god in paradise forever. If you chose to turn away from god, you would not be able to enter the kingdom of heaven. The book of Revelation made it clear what would happen, depending on which path was chosen.

John wrote about god's throne room, which had many signs and symbols from the prophets of the Old Testament, both creatures and elders. The creatures and elders gave praise and worship to god. In god's hand was a scroll that contained the messages of the Old Testament prophets; this scroll outlined how god's kingdom would come to earth as in heaven. The problem was that no one could open the scroll—except for "the Lion of the Tribe of Judah."[64] That is what one of the elders told John, and when John turned, he saw a sacrificial lamb—a symbol of Jesus himself. Jesus

---

63. Revelation 2:7 (AV).
64. Revelation 5:5 (AV).

had conquered evil by dying on the cross; hence, because Jesus gave his life, he was able to open the scroll.

Revelation then mentions the three sets of Divine judgment: the seven seals, the seven trumpets, and the seven bowls. These are seen as series of events that either have taken place, are taking place, or will take place in the future. First, we will examine the seven seals. The lamb (Jesus) opened the first four seals and the four horsemen came. Each of them symbolized a time of war, conquest, famine, and death. The fifth seal represented Christian martyrs and their death. Then the sixth seal was broken, and John described an earthquake and angels with a ring that would mark god's servants that were enduring all of this hardship—144,000 individuals from twelve tribes of Judah, 12,000 from each tribe. Then John saw everyone from every walk of life that had chosen to follow Jesus as their messiah; the innumerable people had become martyrs and died for Jesus. Finally, the seventh seal was broken, but before anything was revealed, the sound of the seven trumpets was heard as a symbol of the cry of the people who suffered in the name of Jesus.

This is where Revelation gets confusing, as John seems to step back and provide another explanation of how the end of times will happen. Now we will examine the seven trumpets. He wrote that god would bring Judgment onto the earth and suffering would continue. The first five trumpet blasts announced the plagues that were placed upon Egypt in the book of Exodus:

1. Water turning to blood

2. Frogs

3. Lice and gnats

4. Swarms of creatures (insects) that were capable of great harm

5. Plague to destroy the livestock

6. Boils to cover both people and livestock

7. Thunderstorms of hail and fire

8. Locusts to cover the earth

9. Darkness for three days

10. The death of the first born[65]

The blast of the sixth trumpet released the four horsemen that came from the first four seals. Then John told a story that the followers of Jesus should tell the nations to turn back to god, and a beast appeared. Depictions of this beast came from the Old Testament book of Daniel. This horrific beast killed the all the followers of Jesus. Next, god brought followers back to life, just like he did with Jesus. At this point, the seventh trumpet sounded and all repented and entered the kingdom of heaven. From this, we see that it is not plagues or judgment that will bring the return of Jesus; it is behaving in a kind and loving way.

Before John reveals what the seven bowls stand for, he begins to speak about the signs in Revelation chapters twelve through fourteen. Cosmic battles are outlined in Revelation 12. Next, an earthly battle to include the beast and the mark of the beast being 666 are outlined in Revelation 13. Finally, in Revelation 14, John speaks about the slain lamb, Jesus, and how the army of followers will create a new kingdom. This is followed by Judgment Day,

---

65. Exodus 7–12 (AV).

where the followers and believers of Jesus will go to heaven and nonbelievers will be crushed out like wine grapes.[66] I remember learning about this when I was a little girl; it was said to be the signs of the end of time.

Now John writes about the seven bowls. Once again, just like with the seven trumpets, the first five bowls pour out the plagues of Egypt as seen above. The sixth bowl pours out the beast mentioned above as well as a dragon who wars against the followers of Jesus in a place called Armageddon. And just like with the seventh trumpet, the seventh bowl pours out the final Judgment Day, and a voice came from the heavens saying, "It is done."[67]

It is good to note that due to the repeated timeline within the seven seals, the seven trumpets, and the seven bowls, some Christians believe that these end times will happen after Jesus returns to earth to save his followers. Others believe the end of times will take place during the time that Jesus returns, and still others believe the end of times will take place before Jesus returns. These are often referred to as post-, during, and pre-apocalypse. Confusing, right? But wait! There is more. If you read Revelation as a vision that is not based in reality, you can easily see that the moral to this story is that the world cannot be saved through judgment nor punishment. The world is saved through a pure, unconditional love that sacrifices everything. I like that message, so I could be down with the Christian end of times story—except for the martyr part. I don't need to be a martyr; been there, done that.

---

66. Revelation 14:19 (AV).
67. Revelation 16:17–21 (AV).

The Norse End of Times Story

Now let's examine the Norse version of the end of times, also known as Ragnarok. In this story we have battles, earthquakes, fire, blood, giant wolves, a large serpent, and Loki. Loki is a remarkably interesting character. He is the worst, until he is not—hard to get a good read on this one.

The Norse end of times story began with Loki playing a significant role in the death of Odin's son, Balder the Bright, who was a favorite of the gods. The Æsir, a group of gods and goddesses, began to look for Loki to bring him to justice, so he hid in a cave that had a waterfall in it. He figured that if anyone came by, he could transform himself into a salmon and swim to the bottom of the waterfall and no one would be the wiser.

However, a member of the Æsir named Kvasir, known to be the wise one, figured out what Loki has done. The gods created a net and Thor dragged the bottom of the water. Loki was caught. The Æsir decided not to kill Loki at this point, but to punish him. They found Odin's son Vali and turned him into a giant wolf. Next Vali, as the wolf, ate Loki's son Narfi. Next, they took Narfi's entrails and used them to tie down Loki in a cave. Skadi, one of the Æsir, found a poisonous snake and hung the snake above Loki so that the venom would drip, one drop at a time, onto Loki's face for eternity. Somehow, Loki's wife, Sigyn, managed to sit with Loki during this time. She used a wooden bowl to catch the snake venom. This worked until the bowl became full and Sigyn needed to empty it, at which point a few drops from the snake landed on Loki's face. This continued for all time throughout eternity—until Ragnarok.

According to the Norse, Ragnarok has not yet occurred. They say Ragnarok begins with three years of long winter. The weather will be harsh and unforgiving, to the point where people are starving and begin to turn on each other. At this point, civilization crumbles—humanity deteriorates. Everyone is dying and/or killing each other. When there are only a few people left, the giant wolves Skoll and Hati—the wolves that are known to chase the sun and moon across the sky—will devour the sun and the moon. The stars will fade, and everything will grow dark and even colder. Next, the earthquakes begin to happen—apocalyptic earthquakes. These huge earthquakes will shift the earth so much that the bonds holding Loki will break. Hence, Loki and his giant wolf named Fenrir will be freed.

Once Loki is free, three roosters will crow. This sound will awaken the giants and all those from the underworld will rise. Additionally, Loki has another son named Jörmungandr, the Midgard Serpent (*Midgard* means earth), who will awaken. He will begin to churn through the seas. Now free, Loki will take his sons (the giant wolf and the serpent), as well as all of the beings from the underworld and the giants, led by Sutr, and go challenge the Æsir in Asgard (the heavenly homes where the Æsir live). There is a bridge that connects Asgard and Midgard (heaven and earth); it is known to be the rainbow bridge, named Bifrost.

So, Loki and all his kindred will work their way across the bridge, and as they do, the bridge will crumble behind them. Heimdall, the Æsir who can see the farthest, will see Loki coming and sound a horn to warn the rest of the Æsir. Odin, the All-Father, will gear up alongside eight hundred of the most honorable dead warriors to face Loki and his army. The battle is on!

Many gods will die at Ragnarok by slaying the monsters that Loki brought. Heimdall and Loki will take each other's lives. Odin will then battle the giant wolf Fenrir; he will take his sword and lodge it in Fenrir's mouth so Fenrir cannot close his mouth. Then Fenrir will swallow Odin.

Then Vidar, one of Odin's sons, will appear on the scene. Vidar has a magick shoe—yes, a shoe. This shoe is so large and indestructible that when Vidar stomps on Fenrir's lower jaw, it will rip his upper jaw off. It is said that Fenrir's bottom jaw touches the earth, and his upper jaw touches the heavens—so that was one huge shoe. Sutr, the giant who led the other giants to Ragnarok, will set all of the worlds on fire and everything will turn to ash.

Yet, there is a silver lining to this story. Because the worlds will be burned down, only water will remain. And in many creation stories, the world comes from the seas and the oceans. Where there is water, there is life. Thus, the worlds will be restored once again.

There are a lot of similarities between the Christian and Norse end of times stories. They are both very dark and not something that you want to think about before you fall asleep; however, these stories show us that at the end of time, a new time begins. One huge difference between the Christian story and the Norse story is that the Christian story only promises a new world for those that are deemed righteous, whereas the Norse story births a new world for all, and so it is with the Hindu and Navajo stories.

The Hindu End of Times Story

In the Hindu end of times story, the fourth age (also known as the Kali Age) begins because of corrupt rulers. Because of corruption, all social order has ended and chaos ensues. In short, this world will be consumed by drought and fire. A storm that lasts for many years will take everything out. After this dark night, it too is followed by the idea that a new age will come. This new age will be created by Vishnu, the god that preserves the Universe, in his form as Lord Kalki, meaning that he keeps the Universe from being destroyed completely. When all is gone and we are left with vast oceans once again, Vishnu will create a new world.

The Navajo End of Times Story

As you have seen in the Navajo stories that we have shared thus far, the concept of moving from one world to another is common. But it is not only moving from one world to another; moreover, it is about moving from one *dimension* to another. As stated previously, the Navajo culture is an oral one due to the fact that the Navajo language has not been a written language for very long. The harsh side of this is as the elders pass away, we are left with fewer and fewer original stories. Additionally, many Navajo people do not like to speak about bad things or bad events. There is a belief system shared among traditional Navajo people that states if you talk about bad things, these bad things will come to you, as you are "calling" them to you as you speak about them. Hence, it is difficult to find an end of times story within the Navajo Nation.

So instead, I will share this wonderful concept with you. There is an ancient Navajo teaching that reveals the purpose of life. It is said that the purpose of life is to continuously grow in our four bodies of existence, and to seek balance as we grow. As simple as this may sound, growth and balance occur in countless ways. Additionally, there is an old Navajo teaching about the sacred number four. Think about how many things can be categorized in fours: directions, seasons, elements, etc. The teaching says the reason that so many basic concepts are sectioned into fours is because we are currently in the third dimension and the natural world is teaching us how to move into the next dimension—the fourth dimension.

▲ ▼ ▲

If you take one thing out of these different end of times stories, I hope it is this: There is no ending without a beginning. There is no night without a morning to follow. There is no ending to the circle—to the cycle. So many legends and lore around the world have this same cyclical nature, reinforcing the idea that after a dark night, a new day will dawn. This is the basic idea of this entire book: there is something beyond what we have become.

Becoming in Science

What does becoming look life from a scientific position? I suppose there are many ways to consider the concept of becoming here. I think that the most logical way is to define the word *becoming*. I would define becoming as the process of moving from one state into another. Hence, the process of what is coming next.

Looking at the end of times through a scientific lens, I would say that the end of times could be indicated by a recession, depression, or the crashing of the stock market, or a natural event (perhaps a pandemic?) that changes the way that mankind conducts its daily life. There are so many examples of the end of specific systems or ideologies, ranging from World Wars, to political systems being challenged and coming to an end, to hurricanes and flooding that wipe out an entire community, to a meteor hitting the earth and causing a great crater, to global warming. Moreover, the ending of these systems and ideologies are always followed by something new—a becoming. After the World Wars, we become a new nation. After political systems are challenged and fall, a revised system becomes the new norm. After a natural disaster, we rebuild and become renewed. This includes a pandemic; we find a new normal.

There are so many examples of this that I will not focus on one. However, like I said previously, there is always life that comes after the ending of a cycle. Just like within many religions and belief systems, we exit the old and step into a new.

Becoming in Tarot

These same concepts can be seen within the Major Arcana in the tarot. The end of times story correlates with the next five cards in the tarot: the Devil and monsters, the Tower and the breaking down of our current structures, the Star bringing new consciousness after destruction, the Moon bringing new inner vision, and the Sun dawning a new day once again.

XV. The Devil

The Devil card in a nutshell: what we attempt to control ends up controlling us. In this card we see Baphomet front and center. Baphomet is a deity that the Knights Templar were accused of worshiping and that subsequently was incorporated into disparate occult and mystical traditions. Traditionally, Baphomet is half woman and half goat. Again, we see one hand is up and the other hand is down—we saw this first in the Magician card and again in the Temperance card. Once again, as above so below. However, in the Magician card, we saw an alchemist working with this magick to create his own destiny. In the Temperance card, we saw an angel bringing in patience. Yet in this card, we see that the wheel rolls both ways; if you are able to bring forth freedom, you are also able to manifest bondage.

It is not the Universe's job to judge what is good or what is bad; the Universe sees all things equally. Human beings are the ones who judge or determine what is considered good and what is deemed bad. It is important to point out that the word *devil* is simply *lived* spelled backward; remove the D and we are left with *evil* and *live*. You can't have one without the other—this is the yin and yang of life. Within one lies the aspect of the other.

On the top of Baphomet's head is an inverted pentagram. I have learned that if the tip of a pentagram is pointing up, this reveals an individual who wants to move up by growing and ascending, and if the tip is pointing down, this reveals an individual whose spirit is pointed downward and has no interest in advancing.

Notice what it is in Baphomet's hand. "The Devil holds fire that points down, in opposition to the nature of fire."[68] Thus, this card represents forces working against nature itself. When one works against nature, one must deal with unnatural phenomenon.

Baphomet is in front of a distinctive black background. Some may suggest that this indicates ignorance or the darkness of the night. I would suggest that it directly correlates with this chapter of the book—the night, or an unknown, unseen environment.

Within the card there is, once again, a male and a female. Are these the same ones from the Lovers card? In most decks, yes! Some suggest that the male and female on this card are Adam and Eve after they fell from grace. Regardless, this card depicts the lower vibration of these two aspects (male and female): sex, drugs, and rock 'n roll! I call this a "golden handcuff." Golden handcuffs are cycles that free you and tie you at the same time; for example, working to buy a nice car but buying a nice car to go to work. On the Lovers card we saw a man and woman standing before an angel; on the Devil card we see them standing before an entity that chains them.

According to Krafchow, the attribute of this card is "foundation" and the keywords are "resisting our nature."[69] Going against the natural flow. Now, whether you subscribe to the idea of a real devil or believe that the devil is something that is a rebellious force is up to you. I do not see either as bad; I see both as the dark night of the soul—the end of times that comes when mankind loses

68. Krafchow, *Kabbalistic Tarot*, chap. 2.
69. Krafchow, *Kabbalistic Tarot*, Tables of Card Associations for Major Arcana.

sight of the natural flow and tries to control the world around them, but the world around them ends up controlling mankind. Another golden handcuff. This is an experience that I would say that most of us, if not all of us, will experience in our lifetime.

The Devil card is ruled by the astrological sign of Capricorn. Capricorn energy is reflected in the energy of cardinal earth. Capricorns are the initiators of material matters and new projects. Have you ever met a Capricorn? Chances are, they have a million new ideas on how to start a project, yet they may not be able to finish these projects. Of course, their follow-through depends on other aspects of their birth chart too. Regardless, we all need to start somewhere when bringing new ideas into the world. If you are having any struggles with this, go talk with a Capricorn—problem solved.

Capricorn is ruled by the planet Saturn. I often say that the planet Saturn feels like old Father Time; a sense of responsibility always tags along with this planet. The chains in the Devil card could correlate with the rings around Saturn. Saturn is the planet of constriction, bondage, and the sense of limitation. As harsh as this energy may seem, I find that it is also very sensitive. Not necessarily in an emotional way, but more in a don't-judge-me-because-I-am-judging-myself-harshly-right-now kind of way.

Because of their high standards, Capricorns are known to be successful in business and in their chosen careers. They are hard workers, high achievers, and very responsible—maybe because they try so hard to prove that they are not going to get caught up in the Devil's game. That is not to say that you'll never meet a lazy, underachieving Capricorn; you very well might meet a Capricorn who lacks responsibility, discipline, and motivation. Encountering people whose qualities are the opposite of their sign happens. Any and all zodiac signs can try to resist their true nature; this is the rebel—the Devil—within us. If you need to find solid footing, you need both the light and the dark to show you where you stand.

XVI. The Tower

Now let's examine the Tower card. Here we find a tower, which is a human-made structure, rather than a structure found in the natural world like a tree or a mountain. A lightning bolt is striking this structure. I see it as a power from above that is breaking down old structures, old beliefs, old ideas, and old ways of doing things. The lightning bolt strikes the crown that was sitting on top of the Tower. I see this crown as the adornment given to mankind when we find material achievements, power, and authority. But now the crown is falling, and authority comes tumbling down.

If you look closely at the card, you can also see a couple of falling figures. Some see these two figures as the man and the woman from the Lovers card that moved into the Devil card, finally released from their captor, yet they are taking a tumble too. However, the figures on this card are fully clothed, which could indicate modesty or concealment. They are falling headfirst, which could indicate a sudden blow that will lead to enlightenment, as seen in the Hanged Man card.

Notice that the Tower was built on a peak—not a very sound foundation. The Tower represents human-made structures, and here we see that all that is human-made will eventually crumble. It reminds me of this quote: "On the day after humans disappear, nature takes over and immediately begins cleaning house—or houses, that is."[70] Without mankind's constant upkeep of structures, the plant and animal kingdoms will reclaim their landscape.

One could also interpret this card to represent the fall of man(kind), just as in the book of Revelation, Ragnarok, and the other end of times stories. Kabbalistically, this card can also be seen as a phallic image getting struck by lightning and blowing off its crown as men jump out the window.[71] Notice that in this interpretation, the men are jumping out of the window rather than falling; "Will is single-minded: Everything else can jump out of the window. Nothing stands before Will."[72] Hence Krafchow states that the attribute of the Tower card is "will" and the keyword is "single-mindedness."[73]

Astrologically, the Tower card is ruled by the planet Mars. Mars is a planet of assertiveness, passion, and even aggression. The sign of Aries is ruled by Mars, and Aries is cardinal fire. Within the Tower card, we see a lot of fire. There are ten flames on one side of the Tower to represent the ten worlds on the Tree of Life. There are twelve flames on the other side to represent the twelve signs of the zodiac. With the fire of Aries and the bolt of lightning from Mars, we are looking at a card that looks like wartime.

Again, let's reflect on the stories that we reviewed earlier in this chapter about war and the end of times. The Tower card is

---

70. Weisman, *The World Without Us*, chap. 2.

71. Krafchow, *Kabbalistic Tarot*, chap. 2.

72. Krafchow, *Kabbalistic Tarot*, chap. 2.

73. Krafchow, *Kabbalistic Tarot*, Tables of Card Associations for Major Arcana.

a deconstruction of old things, things that need to be removed so that we can build new. And so it is with the end of times—one world is destroyed in order for a new world to emerge. What does it take to start a new world? Higher consciousness, as we will see within the next card, the Star.

XVII. The Star

THE STAR.

Even though the human-made world was destroyed in the Tower, the stars, the moon, and the sun will continue shine. Take a moment and consider humanity's relationship with the stars. We have sailors who navigate the sea by looking up at the starry sky. We make wishes upon stars. We watch shooting stars and feel a sense of luck when we see one. And of course, there are numerous astronomers and astrologers who study the night sky.

As we look at the Star card from the Rider-Waite deck, we see one big star front and center. It has radiant energy. It has eight points, which I see as representing the eight cycles of creative energy on earth—the eight sabbats that we roll through each year. Sabbats are considered holy days, and they align with the seasonal calendar and the sun. They align with the equinoxes (fall and spring), the solstices (winter and summer), and the times in between. There are a total of eight sabbats to celebrate. See below, in order:

- **Samhain:** Pronounced sow-en. This is the Celtic New Year. Samhain takes place around October 31. It is when the sun is at 15° Scorpio. Summer has ended, and this is a time to honor the dead and those who have passed.

- **Yule:** Also known as the Winter Solstice. This happens around December 21. It is when the sun is at 1° Capricorn. This is the longest night in the wheel of the year. This is a time when the wheel and the sun stand still. Honor the wheel as it stands still and the moon shines, but remember that the sun will return. From this point forward, the days will lengthen minute by minute for the next six months.

- **Imbolc:** This happens around February 2. It is when the sun is at 15° Aquarius. Here we can celebrate the first milk. The first milk represents newly born livestock and their mothers providing them with their first drink of milk. Additionally, this was when farmers' food supplies were depleting and it was time to focus on the next season of planting. Imbolc is about honoring signs of new growth.

- **Ostara:** This is also known as the Spring Equinox. It happens around March 21. It is when the sun is at 1° Aries. This is a time of fertility, a time when new growth is arriving. In mythology, this is also the time that the goddess returns from the underworld.

- **Beltane:** Some call this May Day. This happens around May 1. It is when the sun is at 15° Taurus. This lands directly between the Spring Solstice and the Summer Solstice. Here one can celebrate the sun as daylight increases and nighttime decreases, as well as celebrate the knowledge that summer is coming. These celebrations may include bonfires where the flames represent the sun.

- **Midsummer:** Also known as the Summer Solstice. This happens around June 21. It is when the sun is at 1° Cancer. This is the longest day of the sun, and from this date onward, nighttime will lengthen until Yule once again.

- **Lammas:** This occurs around August 1. It is when the sun is at 15° Leo. This is a time to celebrate and honor the first harvest. Making a loaf of bread to honor this harvest is a wonderful way to celebrate this time of year.

- **Mabon:** Also known as the Fall Equinox. This happens around September 21. It is when the sun is at 1° Libra. This is a time of celebration and honoring the second harvest. Whereas Lammas celebrates the first harvest, Mabon represents the final harvest of the season.

These eight times of the year that some choose to celebrate align us with the seasons and with the cycles of Mother Earth.

Within the Star card, we can also see smaller stars that have eight points as well. There are seven of them, and I see these as the energy of the seven chakras. These seven stars might also represent the importance of the number seven in the book of Revelation.

Next, we see a woman, who I see as the Great Mother. She is bringing the subconscious energy into the conscious mind. One foot is on the ground and one is in the water, just as we saw in the Temperance card—the balance between two realms.

From a Kabbalistic point of view, the warmth of the Star brings us a sensation of kindness, warmth, and illumination. The brilliance of the sun is obvious to each of us; however, the Star's brilliance is subtle, like a jewel.[74] This starlight energy of illumination is what passes through the woman, and it is poured into the stream of consciousness and upon the earth. According to Krafchow, the attribute of this card is "kindness" and the keywords are "subtle blessing."[75]

From an astrological point of view, the Star card holds Aquarius energy. Aquarius is also known as the water bearer. But Aquarius is an air sign, not a water sign. The type of water that Aquarian energy pours is that of higher consciousness. We also find two pitchers that are pouring out water (consciousness) from the kindness of the stars above into the conscious mind. Aquarius energy is friendly, open-minded, humanitarian, and one step ahead of the rest of us when it comes to brilliant ideas and futuristic thoughts. After the Tower card comes the Star card—after everything falls apart comes a new way of thinking about things. After the world as we know it is destroyed, a new world with higher consciousness grows from it all.

---

74. Krafchow, *Kabbalistic Tarot*, chap. 2.
75. Krafchow, *Kabbalistic Tarot*, Tables of Card Associations for Major Arcana.

XVIII. The Moon

As humankind's self-created world falls, the Moon card invites us into our psyche, both individually and collectively. The Moon invites us to go inward in order to examine where we came from and where we are headed. We are asked to work with the reflective light of the Moon in order to do some self-reflection and introspection.

As we peer into the Moon card, we see a brilliant moon raining down reflective wisdom. Coming out of the water is a shellfish; from the depths of the cosmic conscious mind comes our natural tendency to be examined. This card also has a dog and a wolf. They come from the same family, yet one is domesticated and one is wild, asking us to reflect on both of these aspects within ourselves and within society. Sometimes, in order to move forward, we need to look back to see where we came from.

From a Kabbalistic point of view, the Moon card corresponds to the menstrual cycle. As the cycle comes around, old eggs and old potential are released, and newness begins once again.[76] The ability to let go of the old and step into a new cycle is something that the menstrual cycle reveals to us. According to Krafchow, the attribute of this card is "splendor" and the keywords are "letting go."[77]

From an astrological point of view, the Moon card is ruled by Pisces. I would add that the Moon card also aligns with Cancer,

---

76. Waite, *Pictorial Key to the Tarot*, part II.
77. Krafchow, *Kabbalistic Tarot*, Tables of Card Associations for Major Arcana.

as the moon rules the sign of Cancer. Pisces is ruled by the planet Neptune. As you may recall, when we were looking at the Hermit card, we looked at Neptunian energy. Keywords that describe the planet Neptune are dreams and/or dreamlike states, alternate states of consciousness, illusions, fantasy, the mystical, and psychic energy. Hence, this card is a time to move into a different way of viewing your life and/or the world that we live in. It is a time of deep reflection.

The moon shows us that change is natural within our lives. The moon travels faster than the sun, only taking twenty-eight days to complete a full rotation through all twelve zodiac signs, whereas the sun takes a full year. In many Native American cultures, a menstrual cycle is referred to as a moon cycle.

The Moon card helps us after the Tower has been hit and our world has fallen apart. First we gained higher consciousness in the Star card, then we reflect on this consciousness in the Moon card. What are we going to do with this consciousness and reflection? Well, here comes the Sun.

XIX. The Sun

The sun is both literally and metaphorically a radiant sign of life force energy. The sun is the biggest, the brightest, and the warmest influence on planet Earth. It brings us light so that we can see clearly. The energy of the Sun card is that of coming to Earth to allow things to grow. The face within the Sun card is facing straight forward, whereas the face within the Moon card was looking to the side; the Sun card is a time to look ahead and birth a plan.

Within this card we see sunflowers. Sunflowers always face the sun, rotating each day to catch the most light. This shows us that the earth follows the sun just like the physical realm follows the spiritual realm. We also see a bare child—the golden child, so to speak. I see this as an awakening or being born as the naked truth. There is nothing to hide, only pure innocence as well as simplicity. Some decks will have two children; could this depict the two on the Lovers card, the Devil card, and the Tower card? Some decks may have a feather on the child, like the feather found on the Fool card, the symbol of new beginnings.

The child is riding upon a white horse. I interpret this to represent purity. It is the vehicle of purity that drives the innocence of the child forward. In this card we also see a wall. I see the wall as a human adaptation to structure, yet the wall shows that we are able to find freedom within the structure rather than bondage and limitation. One could say this represents humans trying to figure out which human-made structures can exist without smothering our creative self-expression. Although you may wonder why this card lands in the chapter that addresses the night, the end, and death, it is because the energy from the Sun card is revealing to us that the physical realm should reflect the spiritual realm in order to rise again.

From a Kabbalistic point of view, the Sun card (like the Star card) reveals a type of kindness. In Kabbalah, light is equal to spiritual sustenance, as light holds metaphoric properties of kindness, warmth, and the ability to illuminate everything in its path.[78] This is showing us, once again, that the Sun is spiritual sustenance that is manifest in the earthly realm. According to Krafchow, the attribute of the Sun card is "kindness" and the keywords are "obvious blessings."[79]

Astrologically speaking, the Sun card is ruled by the sun itself. This speaks to me of its wholeness, its ability to bring life back, its brilliance. We measure our day, our year, and our lifetime by the rotation of the sun. The sign of Leo is ruled by the sun. Leos are very warm and shine brightly—when they choose to, of course. There is a feeling of "go big or go home" with Leo energy; I love it! But before we get too carried away with the fun-loving energy, it is judgment time …

XX. Judgement

The Judgement card fits nicely into this section. When we look at the Judgement card in the Rider-Waite deck, we see a great angel in the sky. I see it as Archangel Gabriel, the one in the King James Version of the Christian Bible that sounds the trumpet at the end of the times. From a Kabbalistic point of view, the angel is also identified as Archangel Gabriel.[80]

Gabriel means "the strength of god." In this card, Gabriel stands in the west, the direction where the sun goes down and

---

78. Krafchow, *Kabbalistic Tarot*, chap. 2.

79. Krafchow, *Kabbalistic Tarot*, chap. 2.

80. Krafchow, *Kabbalistic Tarot*, chap. 2.

the end of the day arrives. Gabriel is also known as the one who assists with crossing from one realm to another; he is a psychopomp that guides souls to the realm beyond. The angel blows a great trumpet (which is reflected in the book of Revelation) and is calling for an awakening through sound. There are seven rays of sound coming from the trumpet. These seven rays could also correspond to the seven trumpets in Revelation or the seven seals opening. Or maybe the seven rays depict the awakening of the seven major chakras, or even the seven major musical notes: A, B, C, D, E, F, G—sound and vibration.

This trumpet sound wakes up the human race from what appears to be death. I say this because they are standing in coffins—and I can't think of any other reason why someone would be standing in a coffin that is floating on water. A man, a woman, and a child are looking up from the coffins, with others in the background depicting that there are several individuals, maybe? The man, woman, and child who stand at the forefront of the card can be seen throughout the entire Major Arcana. I am not sure exactly what the water is about; however, I speculate that it has something to do with the river of consciousness we have seen within many of the cards.

Additionally, Krafchow shares that the attribute of this card is "severity" and the keyword is "renewal."[81] I find this interesting because as harsh as death was in the Tower—as harsh as the stories of the end of times were—renewal came afterward. We see the cycle of life, death, and rebirth once again. There is

---

81. Krafchow, *Kabbalistic Tarot*, Tables of Card Associations for Major Arcana.

something after our world, our reality, our position and perspective. Whether it be macro or micro, there is something beyond.

From an astrological point of view, the planet Pluto rules the Judgement card. If you recall, we spoke of Pluto in chapter 3 when we examined the Death card. Pluto represents a greater sense of focused spiritual power and a deep soul capacity that can be brought out and refined. It also holds the energy of death, rejuvenation, and imminent change. Both Pluto and the Judgement card express the sensation of resurrection after death.[82]

▲ ▼ ▲

To wrap up this section on the tarot and how it expresses becoming:

- The Devil card depicts a controlling, human-made system prior to the fall that we see in the next card. It shows a system prior to the cycle of becoming anew.

- The Tower card represents the fall of the human-made system, and thus the need for a new system will develop. This is the fall prior to becoming anew.

- The Star card is the first glimpse of mild light after the Tower. It is an idea of what is to come. This is the first step in the process of becoming anew: an illuminating idea.

- The Moon card is the next step in the process of becoming anew. This step within the process asks

---

82. Kenner, *Tarot and Astrology*, chap. 2.

us to examine our psyche (both individually and collectively).

- The Sun card is the final step in the process of becoming anew. It depicts a system outside of the controlling system that was depicted in the Devil card. Moreover, the Sun represents a new system where we can find freedom.

Again, this is simply another way to explore these concepts. I hope that you are finding this as interesting as I am.

Becoming in Life

At the beginning of this chapter, I shared about how my life has transformed as I've become a young elder. This was my personal story of falling into a peaceful place, a quieter place where I feel more and more settled within myself as I grow older. Also in this chapter, we examined the idea of endings. In my mind, endings are merely a time to let go of something and begin to embrace something new.

This is the cycle coming full circle. The cycle of the morning, noon, evening, and night. The cycle of spring, summer, autumn, and winter. The cycle of birth, adolescence, adulthood, and elder. The cycle of the directions, east, south, west, and north. The cycle of creation, purification, a savior, and an ending of the world as we know it.

These cycles are seen within every walk of life, and within most religions. But we can also see the cycle of asking a question, receiving the answer, applying the answer, and, finally, what manifests from this process.

The Manifestation

The path of the north, the elder, the winter, the night... This is a time when everything has been made manifest. What we manifest comes from the questions that we ask, the answers we receive, and how we apply these answers to our lives. Hence, be aware of what questions you are asking. Be aware of where the answers are coming from; is it a credible source? Be aware of how you are applying the answers to your life. All of this works together to bring forth manifestation in your life.

What types of seeds you plant in your garden and how you tend to your garden will determine what is harvested—what is made manifest. We can manifest many things: a new item, a new relationship, a new job, a new perspective. Some say that the grass is greener on the other side of the fence; however, I say the grass is greener where you water it. How are tending to your garden?

Think about the process shown to us by the butterfly. It has four stages, and it looks different at every stage. The egg stage is the idea stage—the question. The caterpillar stage is the research stage—the answer. The cocoon stage is the time to go within and consider what the end product will look like—the application. Finally, the butterfly is born—the manifestation.

Journal Prompts for Becoming

In this section, I will provide you with prompts so that you can consider how you experience the world around you. I invite you to record your responses to these prompts in a journal. You could even use these prompts to start a conversation with others!

1) When you think of the word *becoming*, what comes to your mind?

2) How do you experience becoming? That is to say, what does becoming look like to you within each of your four bodies of existence?

   - Physical body

   - Emotional body

   - Mental body

   - Spiritual body

3) In the section Becoming in the Natural World, we discussed how becoming is like the nighttime, wintertime, and elder years. Even if you are not an elder yet, think about what the word *elder* means to you. This is simply a jumping-off point for you to think about what each of these means to you. Take a moment and personalize it. How would you describe each of these?

   Take a moment and brainstorm descriptions of what the night brings. If you find yourself stuck, I have started a list, but I encourage you to take some time and contemplate what the night means to you personally.

   - There is nothing as comfortable as a soft pillow after a long day. May I close my eyes and experience a night of deep, restful step.

- I am finished with the morning, the noontime, and the evening. I have earned a good,
peaceful sleep.

- May my mind dream, and in these dreams,
may I understand myself and others more.
May I allow my spirit to soar and show me
a tomorrow full of beauty. I will rest so that
whatever tomorrow brings, I will be ready.

Writing these depictions helps the night feel
more alive. Take a few moments to think about or
write down what you experience during the night.
There is almost a poetic vibe to this experience.
Once you have written a few sentences describing the night, look at what you have written and
change the word *night* to *becoming*. How does that
affect what you wrote?

4) In the section Becoming in Tarot, we discussed six
tarot cards. Now, you can step into the cards and
personalize each of them: the Devil, the Tower,
the Star, the Moon, the Sun, and Judgement. Here
is how to do this:

- Take a look at each card individually and
write down what pops out to you. What
does that item or person look like to you?
What meaning does it hold for you? What
do you see? Write this down.

- Step into the card. Use your imagination to
become one of the characters within the

card. From that position, what do you see? What do you feel like? Can you identify with this character? If so, how do you identify with this character? Write it down.

- Feel into your four bodies. Once you have stepped into the card, go a little deeper into the card by noticing the following:

  - What does your physical body sense? Is it relaxed, tight, cold, or warm?

  - What does your emotional body feel? Is it happy, sad, confused, or uplifted?

  - What does your mental body pick up on? Does it feel wonder or enlightenment, or do you hear any words?

  - What does your spiritual body experience? Does it feel empowered or trapped, or does it feel a sense of purpose? If it is difficult for you to extract what your spiritual body is experiencing, I recommend looking at what you wrote down for the other bodies and extract the overarching theme.

5) What are your thoughts on manifestation? In chapter 1, we discussed asking questions. Chapter 2 was about receiving the answer to these questions, and chapter 3 was about application. Now it is time to reflect on manifestation; what does that look like to you?

6) Upon completing prompts one through five, extract the overarching concepts. At this point, you can write a story, a poem, or even a few sentences to assist you in personalizing what becoming means to you.

5

BEYOND
(A NEW DAY)

When I was a little girl, I had a great fear. It was not an ordinary fear, such as a monster under the bed or in the closet. If you haven't noticed by now, I am a different breed. My greatest fear was the concept of tomorrow. I remember lying in bed, crying myself to sleep because I didn't know what would come tomorrow. Plus, I was so tired from today—how was I to face tomorrow too? One night, as I was scared and crying under the covers, a thought came to me. *Am I afraid of today? No. So, if I always stay in the idea of today, tomorrow will never come.* See, the word *tomorrow* implies something different—a different experience, a different world—is on the horizon. So I gave up the concept of tomorrow, and the problem was solved.

As silly as that story may sound, there is a deeper meaning here. This chapter is about the idea of tomorrow: what will happen after today is over. I believe we will move into another experience, just like we have moved through this day, this year, this lifetime. There are many thoughts, ideas, and beliefs about the afterlife; there are even stories of near-death experiences that have been shared all over the world. I am not here to ask you to believe in one thing in particular. Instead, in this chapter we are going to examine various ideas in order to expand our own thoughts of the beyond.

Beyond in My Life

What lies beyond? What does life look like after elderhood? For me, the beyond is about carrying on a legacy that has been passed down for many generations: spirituality and the choice to be a spiritual leader. From my ancestors to me, and from me to future generations. I am not only speaking of sharing my legacy with members of my bloodline. I am speaking of sharing my legacy with any and all individuals who are inspired, encouraged, and empowered to be their authentic self. If I can play even the smallest role in that process, I will have lived a wonderful life.

Additionally, another thing that lies beyond me that came from me is the Eagle Heart Foundation. I am currently the founding CEO; in my eyes, my job is to build an organization that will outlive me—something that extends beyond me. To be even the smallest part of something wonderful that brings hope, love, education, understanding, and compassion to others... this is what lies beyond me.

I envision a world that promotes authenticity.

I envision a world that welcomes differences.

I envision a world that will seek to understand.

I envision a world that will embrace the unknown—that embraces the beyond.

I envision a world where we will all celebrate ourselves!

Beyond in the Four Bodies

What does the concept of beyond look like in each of the four bodies of existence? In this section, I will begin that conversation with you. However, this section is just a jumping-off point; I would like you to think about how you personally experience the beyond in the four bodies. There will be a journal prompt at the end of the chapter that can help you with this.

Within the physical body, when I travel to a place that I have not been before, my body becomes alert and aware. It is like I am experiencing an awakening. I am going beyond the places I have traveled to before. My five senses become aware of new land, and I move within this new land with curiosity. I question how to interact with this new land.

Within the emotional body, the beyond is experiencing a new emotional state. Again, it is an awakening, as we discussed earlier in the book. When you fall in love for the very first time, you have gone beyond the emotions that you once knew. You are in a more expansive or expressive emotional state. Sometimes moving beyond within the emotional body can be uncomfortable. Experiencing unfamiliar emotions can create a little anxiety; however, when we relax and let the emotions come, we slowly realize that experiencing new emotions expands our emotional body's awareness. Hope is the emotion that can place us in an emotional state beyond our current state. Another way to experience the beyond is through empathy; feeling empathy for another is the act of moving beyond your emotions into someone else's emotional state.

In the mental body, beyond is the concept of thinking outside of the way that you currently think. Maybe you experience another person's worldview or thought process while reading a good book or watching a powerful movie. The simplest way to move beyond within the mental realm is the act of listening. Step into another person's shoes and consider the world around them as they see it. When you are a good listener, you are moving beyond your mental body and stepping into another's mental body, bringing connectedness and understanding. I try to do this often.

In the spiritual body, I would say that the beyond is another awakening. You move beyond what you are currently experiencing and into something deeper, something broader, something more defined, something else. There comes a moment within the spiritual body when everything feels like it makes sense—and then, in the next moment, you find out there is more to learn. This is the ever-awakening, endlessly unfolding lotus within each of us.

Beyond in the Natural World

When we are examining the natural world, we are viewing the overarching concept of each chapter within a day, a year, and a lifetime. What is beyond a day? Tomorrow. Although tomorrow shares similarities with today—such as the sun rising in the east and setting in the west—there will be differences each new day. Noticing the subtle differences within each day allows you to appreciate each day in the cycle of the year.

One year moves into another year, and this cycle continues beyond our lifetime. Again, both contentedness and newness can be found in these familiar cycles. For example, we know that weather patterns continue throughout the seasons, but each season can be experienced differently depending on where you are in your life cycle. Moreover, what comes at the end of a life cycle?

Your lineage and your legacy. Hence, I ask myself to do things in my life that will leave a positive impression on the future human race. As large or small as this is, each of us has the ability to do this within our lifetime.

The natural world tells us that life doesn't move in a linear motion. Life is cyclical. Hence, the concept of beyond within the natural world simply means it is the next step in the cycle. Yes, sometimes the circle of life changes slightly—we can see in the natural world—so maybe I should describe this as less of a circle and more of a spiral. If you observe a spiral from the top looking downward, it looks like a circle. However, if you observe a spiral from the side, you see that it moves up and down in a circular fashion. So the spiral represents life's cyclical nature that is full of ups and downs.

Beyond in Religion

What lies beyond? Is there life after the end of times? Is there life after death? Well, I suppose that depends on what belief system you have. In this section, we are going to look at this from the perspectives of Christianity, Norse lore, and traditional Navajo stories. I will go into more detail soon, but first, allow me to provide a brief overview of the stories we are going to examine:

- In Christianity, the beyond is called heaven.

- In Norse lore, the beyond is a new world, a world that is called Midgard (Earth).

- In the traditional Navajo stories, once we learn all there is to know from one world, we will emerge into the next world.

The Christian Beyond

In the Christian faith, and in many other belief systems, there is a place called heaven. Heaven has pearly gates and streets of gold. In this place there is no sadness, there is no strife, there is no death. There is no war—the lion lies down with the lamb. In order to get into this place, you must believe in Jesus and ask him to save you. If you do not, well ... fire and brimstone for you. Heaven sounds like a lovely place, situated beyond the clouds. You get to see old family members and friends. And if you believe that animals go to heaven—well, I have a bunch of cats and dogs that are waiting for me there.

Does this place exist? Here is what I think. If you believe in it, it does exist. I believe that those who believe in such a place will go to this wonderful place, as their consciousness will create this. I think anyone who desires heaven will find it. I don't think I will make it there. Maybe a part of me will make it to heaven—the part of me that my Christian elders hold within their memory. That aspect of me will join them beyond the pearly gates.

The Norse Beyond

What happens if you do not believe in the heavenly place of final resting? There are so many other beliefs to consider. In my studying of the Norse lore, I found that something does come post-Ragnarok. A new world is created from the bodies of water that survived the ashy destruction. The sons and daughters of the elder gods will bring forth a new world. Once again, everything will be restored in a new world, but they do not call it heaven. Midgard (Earth) is created once again. The Norse see the beyond as the dawning of a new day—a new age.

The Navajo Beyond

As we've discussed since the beginning of this book, the Navajo believe that once we learn all there is to learn within one world, we will emerge into the next world—a process of life, death, and rebirth. Think of corn fields. After all of the fields are harvested in autumn and the ground is put to rest for the winter, new seeds will be planted in fields and the cycle begins again. This is a micro idea of a macro concept. This cycle applies not only to our individual lives, but to the lifespan of humanity.

▲ ▼ ▲

If you take one thing out of these different beyond stories, I hope it is that there is always more. There is always a tomorrow. There is always a next season. There is always a continuation of existence. Even if you believe that nothing comes after death, you will still exist within the hearts and memories of those who love you. Your life affects us all in one way or another.

Beyond in Science

Keeping in good form, let's look at what is beyond from a scientific perspective. Albert Einstein is known to have said that energy cannot be created nor destroyed. However, it simply changes into something else. I think this says it all. Life as we know it may change, but life never dies.

We can also look at the history of mankind and some of the turning points in history—our ages. Although I am not a history buff, I have heard terms such as the Paleolithic Era and the Neolithic Era. Also, we have the Stone Age, the Bronze Age, and the Iron Age. More modern history has the Atomic Age, Space Age, and Information Age. Are you noticing that something always lies beyond? When one age is complete, we step into a new one.

Another way to look at the concept of beyond within science is what is beyond Mother Earth. The sun, the moon, and the stars are beyond Earth. The night sky and technology reveal to us that there are other planets in our solar system. Additionally, when we look at the bigger picture, we find that there are other solar systems. When we look even further, we see that we are part of the Milky Way galaxy. Beyond that, astronomers who study deep, distant space have found other galaxies too. More galaxies than we can count. From there it simply continues to go beyond. *Beyond* appears to be endless.

Beyond in Tarot

We have moved through all the Major Arcana cards except for the final card within the deck.

XXI. The World

The World card is the balance between all the elements and astrological signs. It is the completed cycle. There is one central figure in this card. The legs look to be in the same position as they were in the Hanged Man card. This figure has achieved enlightenment and has the ability to manifest consciously. Maybe this card represents the manifestation of the enlightenment that was received by the Hanged Man. Could this card be "the state of the restored world when the law of manifestation shall have been carried to the highest degree of natural perfection"?[83]

In the Rider-Waite version of this card, the central figure appears to be dancing or levitating, loosely wrapped in a veil. I wonder if this depicts the ability to dance with the veil? Does it depict that there is more to be seen than what is obvious? Dancing with two wands makes me think about the dualities that we have within this world and how those two opposites can find a happy balance. The balance between involution and evolution. Not only as above, so below; moreover, as within, so without. Manifestation in all forms. This card also has an evergreen wreath that encircles the figure, which speaks to me of everlasting life, things coming full circle, the cycle of life—and the cycle of tarot, as we will return to the Fool card once again.

Just as we saw in the Wheel of Fortune card, this card has four symbols, one in each corner. In one corner is a man; another corner has an eagle; in another corner, there is a bull; and in the last corner, there is a lion. These images are directly correlated to the four fixed signs of the zodiac. The man represents fixed air, Aquarius. The eagle represents fixed water, Scorpio. (It is said that when the scorpion has reached maturity, it evolves and transforms into an eagle.) The bull represents fixed earth, Taurus. Finally, the lion represents fixed fire, Leo. This card is a representation of air, water, earth, and fire—the four elements working together in harmony to manifest good things.

Kabbalistically, the World card represents that what is spoken from above (from the heavens) makes things manifest in

---

83. Waite, *Pictorial Key to the Tarot*, part II.

the physical realm.[84] Could this card indicate the meeting of the above and below, the heaven and earth, the within and without, all in one? According to Krafchow, the attribute of this card is "speech" and the keywords are "observable speech of the Creator."[85] Again, we see a circle—a cycle—for it was with words that god created the heavens and the earth in the beginning.

Astrologically, the World card is aligned with the planet Saturn. Good old Father Time. We have examined Saturn a couple of times within this book—under the Devil card and the Justice card. So, how do we correlate the World card with the planet Saturn? One way to look at it that there are rings around Saturn, which can indicate the boundaries and limitations that we experience in life. But the World card has a wreath around the central figure, which shows us that the limitations and boundaries that we adopt will eventually provide us with freedom and everlasting life. Although we may live in a world of endless possibilities, Saturn assists us in understanding that a wise individual will also recognize their limits.[86] It is a sort of reality check for us. We must remember all of the lessons that we've learned and make healthier choices for the world that is to come—what lies beyond.

This is the whole cycle! We are more similar than we are different. I look at a world where so many people think in terms of separation. So many people solidify themselves as being different than another. I, too, am different—but I can find common ground with every human on earth. There are so many similarities in our daily cycle of light and dark, in our yearly cycle of the

---

84. Krafchow, *Kabbalistic Tarot*, chap. 2.

85. Krafchow, *Kabbalistic Tarot*, Tables of Card Associations for Major Arcana.

86. Kenner, *Tarot and Astrology*, chap. 2.

seasons, in our life cycles, and in our beliefs. We are all more alike than we may realize.

Beyond in Life

At the beginning of this chapter, I shared my personal thoughts about what lies beyond my life. I shared that I do my best to live a life that will produce a positive world for the next generations. The grand cycle continues beyond me.

Repeat the Cycle

We began with a question. Once a question is asked, there is almost a magnetic draw to the answer. Once the answer arrives, we must address the answer. Addressing the answer causes us to take action on whatever it is that we are asking about. Once we respond to the answer through application, we manifest. So what comes after this? Another question.

At the beginning of this book, I mentioned that when I was a little girl, I was told not to ask questions. At this point in my life, I see how harmful that can be. If we don't ask questions, we lose answers and the ability to manifest an authentic life. If we don't ask questions, how can we evolve?

Some call me a teacher, but I call myself a student of life who enjoys sharing what I have found. If in my sharing, I am teaching, so be it. However, I approach life with curiosity, which leads me to more and more questions. These questions receive answers, and I go from there. Through this process, I continue to grow and expand. When I am in a difficult situation, I step back from all of the assumptions that I am making and ask questions. This opens my mind, opens my heart, and opens my spirit, and I evolve.

Journal Prompts for Beyond

In this section, I will provide you with prompts so that you can consider how you experience the world around you. I invite you to record your responses to these prompts in a journal. You could even use these prompts to start a conversation with others!

1) When you think of the word *beyond*, what comes to your mind?

2) How do you experience the beyond? That is to say, what does the beyond look like to you within each of your four bodies of existence?

    • Physical body

    • Emotional body

    • Mental body

    • Spiritual body

3) In the section Beyond in the Natural World, we discussed how the beyond is like the tomorrow, the next year, and the afterlife. This is simply a jumping-off point for you to think about what each of these means to you. Take a moment and personalize it. How would you describe each of these concepts?

    Take a moment and brainstorm what tomorrow brings. If you find yourself stuck, I have started a list, but I encourage you to take some time and contemplate what tomorrow means to you personally.

- Tomorrow brings another opportunity for me to learn something new.

- Tomorrow brings with it new adventures, and possibly new ideas as well.

- Tomorrow I will feel refreshed once again, and it is my intention to approach my world, my life, and myself with more love and compassion.

Writing these depictions helps tomorrow feel more alive. Take a few moments to think about or write down what you experience when you think about tomorrow. There is almost a poetic vibe to this experience. Once you have written a few sentences describing tomorrow, look at what you have written and change the word *tomorrow* to *beyond*. How does that affect what you wrote?

4) In the section Beyond in Tarot, we discussed one tarot card. Now, you can step into the World card and personalize it. Here is an exercise on how to do this:

- Take a look at the card and write down what pops out to you. What does that item or person look like to you? What meaning does it hold for you? What do you see? Write this down.

- Step into the card. Use your imagination to become one of the characters within the card. From that position, what do you see?

What do you feel like? Can you identify with this character? If so, how do you identify with this character? Write it down.

- Feel into your four bodies. Once you have stepped into the card, go a little deeper into the card by noticing the following:

  ◦ What does your physical body sense? Is it relaxed, tight, cold, or warm?

  ◦ What does your emotional body feel? Is it happy, sad, confused, or uplifted?

  ◦ What does your mental body pick up on? Does it feel wonder or enlightenment, or do you hear any words?

  ◦ What does your spiritual body experience? Does it feel empowered or trapped, or does it feel a sense of purpose? If it is difficult for you to extract what your spiritual body is experiencing, I recommend looking at what you wrote down for the other bodies and extract the overarching theme.

5) Upon completing prompts one through four, extract the overarching concepts. At this point, you can write a story, a poem, or even a few sentences that will assist you in personalizing what beyond means to you.

CONCLUSION

In the introduction, I shared my personal story of splitting from my family at the age of seventeen because I questioned their religious beliefs. This led to the end of our relationship. I wonder what would have happened if the beliefs of my biological family would have been more adaptable to my authenticity. I also wonder how many people have been negatively impacted by the closed-mindedness of others. Can our beliefs be so strong that, if challenged, we will go to war to defend them? Yes. Can our beliefs be so strong that, if crossed, we lose friends and family who disagree? Yes. Do our belief systems truly dictate how we move in the world and how we respond to the world? Yes. But— what if what we believe is out of date? What if there is something beyond what we perceive, both individually and collectively?

Before we can dive into that, let's examine the concept of perception. Perception happens within the mind, not within the eye. There is scientific evidence of this. "The place where the optic nerve goes through the eyeball to the back of the brain has no visual receptors."[87] It is the *brain* that is perceiving. Moreover, think about this: a visually impaired or sight-impaired individual still perceives the world around them. Our eyes are not as crucial to perception as you may think.

This has been demonstrated time and time again with science. In one study, scientists measured the electrical output of an individual's brain with a CAT scan while they looked at an object. Next, they asked the individual to close their eyes and visualize the object. Both times—whether the person saw the object with their own eyes or imagined it in their mind's eye—the same areas of the brain were activated and putting out electrical pulses.[88]

So, it is safe to say that the brain doesn't necessarily distinguish what it sees within an external environment and what it imagines.[89] Additionally, scientific evidence also shows us that the physical body doesn't seem to know the difference between an action performed and the same action visualized.[90] Hence, there is science that backs up the idea that visualization can be a key technique for high-performing individuals. Visualization and manifestation go hand in hand. Creating a vision board helps our bodies and minds perceive ourselves in a different situation. Once we've achieved visualization, we then take small steps and actions to get to that destination.

But wait. If eyesight isn't a crucial part of perception, how do we perceive? What is happening within the mind if the eyes are not actually seeing? According to science, when we look at things,

---

87. Arntz, Chasse, and Vicente, *What the Bleep Do We Know?!*, chap. 6.
88. Arntz, Chasse, and Vicente, *What the Bleep Do We Know?!*, chap. 6.
89. Arntz, Chasse, and Vicente, *What the Bleep Do We Know?!*, chap. 6.
90. Arntz, Chasse, and Vicente, *What the Bleep Do We Know?!*, chap. 6.

we perceive impulses of shapes, colors, and patterns. Next, we match these patterns with our stored memories, relating them to past stories, and experience an emotion around these stories. Finally, we assign a meaning to what we are perceiving. Then, like a flashing movie show, our brain flashes "picture frames" of what we are perceiving at the rate of forty times a second. Which means that we are not seeing continuously—the brain is rapidly showing us pictures.[91] This is the process of perception in the brain. This is how your brain perceives, even as you are reading the pages of this book.

In short, perception is perceiving patterns and aligning them with stored memory. But what happens if we are viewing something that we have never seen before? What does the mind do? If we see something that we have never seen before, one of two things will happen. Either we will find something within our memory to compare it to in order to comprehend what we are viewing, or our brain will literally block the image from our mind, giving us a blind spot. Research shows us that our mind pulls in information from our senses at the rate of about 400 billion bits per second, yet we only process around 2,000 bits per second.[92] The filtration system of what we receive versus what we perceive is staggering. As our minds are assigning us a plausible story to the phenomenon that we are experiencing, there is room for a lot of extra information to be dumped.[93] And if our

91. Arntz, Chasse, and Vicente, *What the Bleep Do We Know?!*, chap. 6.
92. Arntz, Chasse, and Vicente, *What the Bleep Do We Know?!*, chap. 6.
93. Arntz, Chasse, and Vicente, *What the Bleep Do We Know?!*, chap. 6.

mind cannot make sense of what we just saw, we dismiss what we saw as though we simply imagined it. [94]

Only a fool believes that he doesn't have any blind spots. We all have blind spots within our perception, within our minds. I know I do! One year, I went through a handful of surgeries on both of my wrists. I was down for the count. I couldn't open a jar of food, let alone drive or work during this time. (Good thing I had a good job and great insurance.) I took this time to study the idea of perception. I began to say a mantra several times a day: "Let me perceive what is truly before me." Then I began to have very strange experiences. For example, I saw blue and green lights within the night sky, like the aurora borealis. This might not sound crazy to a person who lives in Alaska, but I live in Colorado, and we don't see the northern lights here. Was I seeing reflections of the lights of the city? Or was I seeing something else? To this day, I do not know—and to this day, I still see strange phenomenon in my day-to-day activity. I simply learned to accept what I cannot explain—to accept my blind spots—and my mind opened even more to the idea that there is something beyond.

I want to clarify that we do not experience perception's blind spots as holes or darkness within the visual field. We fill in our blind spots. Hence, we don't even recognize that we have a blind spot until it is too late. Think about blind spots in terms of driving. When I am driving and try to check my blind spots, I do not experience a black spot within my vision. My mind fills in the blanks. You can't tell you have a blind spot, but we all have them.

---

94. Arntz, Chasse, and Vicente, *What the Bleep Do We Know?!*, chap. 6.

I learned about the concept of blind spots when learning how to drive a car. As I was learning how to drive, I was repeatedly told to check my blind spots, the areas around the car that your mirrors cannot show you, especially when changing lanes. "Look for cars," my driving instructor would say, "Look for cars." Years later I heard that if you are only looking for a car in your blind spot, you will miss the motorcycle that is right there. Why? Because your mind is not looking for motorcycles—your mind is looking for cars. My husband confirmed this. He told me that when he was learning how to ride a motorcycle, the instructor told the class, "People on motorcycles are invisible, so drive as though the people in the cars cannot see you."

As we've discussed, perception is not only visible, so neither are blind spots. I would like to expand and explore the concept of blind spots in other areas of our perceived world. Have you ever witnessed someone who is not able to "read the room"? They seem to be totally oblivious to social signals that people are uncomfortable, or they don't pick up on the fact that they are speaking too long and people are bored. This is a form of a blind spot as well. How about the individual who doesn't realize that you want to get off of the phone, so they keep talking? Again, a social blind spot. How about the person who is so focused on their work that they don't realize you are standing there and would like to ask a question? You can recognize that they are focused on something and try not to take it personally, but it still might seem rude. Blind spot.

I once dated a guy who had emotional blind spots. He used very harsh language and stomped around and then wondered why I would not open up to him. So we can have emotional blind spots and social blind spots. What other types of blind spots can you think of?

One of the biggest blind spots I see in the world is the individual who refuses to look outside of their own belief system. Moreover, they refuse to acknowledge that they have blind spots. When we as a society have blind spots that we ignore, it can be very harmful to others. This can cause prejudice and a lack of empathy for marginalized groups. One could argue that social blind spots are what create and sustain marginalized groups, whether we are speaking about people of a different skin color, people who have a different sexual orientation, people who do not have the same religious path, or simply individuals whom we don't see as equal. For this reason, I wrote this book. I have been harmed by blind spots. I seek not to harm others with my blind spots. And to begin to work on your blind spots, you must first realize you have them.

I know I have blind spots. There is no shame in having a blind spot. Recognizing that we all have blind spots allows us to relax and open up to another person's perception and perspective. It is okay not to know something. So I invite you to start asking more and more questions to fill in more and more of your blind spots. And I will do the same.

Again, when we ask questions, we receive answers. When we apply what we have learned from the answer, we manifest a world that we can all enjoy, a world that is a little more open-minded for all of us to express our authenticity.

My friends would say that I am an open-minded individual, but this does not mean that I adopt every thought, every walk of life, and every belief system presented to me. Instead, I am open-minded because I understand that everyone has the right to be who and what they are. I do not have to be like someone in order to understand them. I am me and you are you—that's the way it should be!

I do hope that you have enjoyed the concepts within this book. May this book lead you to more self-discovery.

May we awaken and ask questions.

May these questions lead us to enlightenment as we find answers.

May we apply these answers to our story and be our own hero.

May we manifest based on this journey and let go of the old that no longer serves us.

May we complete this cycle and begin once again.

May we be open enough to understand that there is something beyond our own belief system, our own experience, our own perspective, so that we do not shut the door on another.

May we open ourselves up to give and receive more love.

May we fearlessly explore the world and the beyond!

MAJOR ARCANA QUICK REFERENCE

0. The Fool	
Element	Air
Planetary Ruler	Uranus
Astrological Correspondence	Aquarius
Messages	New beginnings, leap of faith, the awakening, trust versus fear
Qualities	Innocence, unlimited new possibilities, adventure

I. The Magician	
Element	Air
Planetary Ruler	Mercury
Astrological Correspondence	Gemini, Virgo
Messages	Ability to manifest, as above so below, as within so without
Qualities	Ingenuity, working with all the tools, alchemist, wizard

II. The High Priestess	
Element	Water
Planetary Ruler	Moon
Astrological Correspondence	Cancer
Messages	Intuition, sensitivities, esoteric knowledge and/or hidden wisdoms
Qualities	Oracle, spiritual guidance, subconscious

III. The Empress	
Element	Air
Planetary Ruler	Venus
Astrological Correspondence	Libra
Messages	Success and wealth through feminine empowerment and fertility
Qualities	Feminine creator, mother of ideas, love, etc.

IV. The Emperor	
Element	Fire
Planetary Ruler	Mars
Astrological Correspondence	Aries
Messages	Wealth and stability through masculine empowerment
Qualities	Authority, leadership, governance

V. The Hierophant	
Element	Earth
Planetary Ruler	Venus
Astrological Correspondence	Taurus
Messages	Reverend, orthodox and/or traditional, practical versus unconventional
Qualities	Inner teacher or master, organization, conformist

VI. The Lovers	
Element	Air
Planetary Ruler	Mercury (with Venus influence)
Astrological Correspondence	Gemini
Messages	Harmony, love, romantic and sexual connection
Qualities	Male and female combination

VII. The Chariot	
Element	Water
Planetary Ruler	Moon (with Jupiter Influence)
Astrological Correspondence	Cancer, Sagittarius
Messages	Balanced forward movement, victory, activity
Qualities	Champion, vehicle for progress and spirit

VIII. Strength	
Element	Fire
Planetary Ruler	Sun, Neptune
Astrological Correspondence	Leo
Messages	Strength, empowerment, higher self versus ego self
Qualities	Balance between severity and mercy, fortitude

IX. The Hermit	
Element	Earth
Planetary Ruler	Mercury
Astrological Correspondence	Virgo (with Aquarius influence)
Messages	Inner knowing, meditation, introspection
Qualities	Higher guidance, discretion, supreme higher will

X. Wheel of Fortune	
Element	Fire
Planetary Ruler	Jupiter (with Uranus influence)
Astrological Correspondence	Sagittarius
Messages	Destiny, cycles and rotation, fortune, lady luck
Qualities	Cosmic law of karma, everything responds to sequential law

XI. Justice	
Element	Air
Planetary Ruler	Venus (with Saturn influence)
Astrological Correspondence	Libra (with Capricorn influence)
Messages	Balance, fairness, virtue
Qualities	Integrity, harmony, balanced scales

XII. The Hanged Man	
Element	Water
Planetary Ruler	Neptune
Astrological Correspondence	Pisces
Messages	Surrender and sacrifice, illumination through letting go
Qualities	Wisdom gained through sacrifice

XIII. Death	
Element	Water
Planetary Ruler	Mars (with Pluto and Uranus influence)
Astrological Correspondence	Scorpio
Messages	Great transition or transformation
Qualities	Change, releasing the old, letting go

XIV. Temperance	
Element	Fire
Planetary Ruler	Jupiter
Astrological Correspondence	Sagittarius
Messages	Patience, equilibrium, tolerance for ambiguity
Qualities	Filling your own cup, moderation, self-control

XV. The Devil	
Element	Earth (with fire influence)
Planetary Ruler	Saturn (with Mars influence)
Astrological Correspondence	Capricorn
Messages	Bondage, what we control ends up controlling us
Qualities	The lower vibration

XVI. The Tower	
Element	Fire, water
Planetary Ruler	Mars
Astrological Correspondence	Aries, Scorpio
Messages	Deconstruction
Qualities	The point when we are asked to release the old in order for the new to come in

XVII. The Star	
Element	Air
Planetary Ruler	Uranus
Astrological Correspondence	Aquarius
Messages	Internal and external balance
Qualities	Mediation, insight, hope and joy for a new day of consciousness

XVIII. The Moon	
Element	Water
Planetary Ruler	Moon, Neptune
Astrological Correspondence	Cancer, Pisces
Messages	Inner wisdom will come from the depths
Qualities	Meditation, reflection, introspection

XIX. The Sun	
Element	Fire
Planetary Ruler	Sun
Astrological Correspondence	Leo
Messages	Spiritual awakening, things coming to light, success
Qualities	New beginnings, accomplishments, happiness

XX. Judgement	
Element	Fire
Planetary Ruler	Pluto
Astrological Correspondence	Scorpio
Messages	Discernment
Qualities	Making the right decisions

XXI. The World	
Element	Earth
Planetary Ruler	Saturn
Astrological Correspondence	Capricorn (with Libra influence)
Messages	The Magician exalted, the world is at your feet
Qualities	Completion and cosmic consciousness, the complete cycle

OVERALL MATRIX

Awakening (Inspires a belief)	Enlightenment (Reinforces a belief)	Being (Belief impacts what we are)	Becoming (Belief impacts what we will become)
Morning	Noon	Evening	Night
East	South	West	North
Spring	Summer	Autumn	Winter
Childhood	Adolescence	Adulthood	Elderhood
Creation	The flood	The savior/hero	The end of times
The question	The answer	The application	The manifestation

BIBLIOGRAPHY

Benjamin, Ludy T. "The Birth of American Intelligence Testing." *Monitor on Psychology* 40, no. 1 (January 2008): 20. https://www.apa.org/monitor/2009/01/assessment.

Bohm, David, and Robert A. Weinberg. *On Dialogue*. New York: Routledge, 1996.

Bretz, J. Harlen. "The Spokane Flood Beyond the Channeled Scablands." *The Journal of Geology* 33, no. 2 (February–March 1925): 97–115. https://doi.org/10.1086/623179.

Campbell, Joseph. *The Hero with a Thousand Faces*. Novato, CA: New World Library, 2008.

Friedman, Thomas L. *Thank You for Being Late: An Optimist's Guide to Thriving in the Age of Accelerations*. New York: Picador, 2017.

Gardner, Howard. *Multiple Intelligences*. New York: Basic Books, 2006.

Godin, M. Leona. *There Plant Eyes: A Personal and Cultural History of Blindness*. New York: Pantheon Books, 2021.

Kenner, Corrine. *Tarot and Astrology: Enhance Your Readings with the Wisdom of the Zodiac*. Woodbury, MN: Llewellyn, 2012.

Koneya, Mele, and Alton Barbour. *Louder Than Words: Nonverbal Communication*. Columbus, OH: Merrill, 1976.

Krafchow, Dovid. *Kabbalistic Tarot: Hebraic Wisdom in the Major and Minor Arcana*. Rochester, VT: Inner Traditions, 2005. Kindle.

Leeming, David Adams. *The World of Myth*. Oxford: Oxford University Press, 1991.

McGee, Gary Z. "Joseph Campbell's Four Basic Functions of Mythology." Fractal Enlightenment. Accessed September 21, 2021. https://fractalenlightenment.com/36315/life/joseph-campbells-four-basic-functions-of-mythology.

RavenWolf, Silver. *Solitary Witch: The Ultimate Book of Shadows for the New Generation*. Woodbury, MN: Llewellyn Publications, 2009.

Shakespeare, William. *The Complete Works of William Shakespeare*. London: Wordsworth Edition Limited, 2007.

Waite, Arthur Edward. *The Pictorial Key to the Tarot*. Santa Cruz, CA: BLTC Press, 2007. Kindle.

Weisman, Alan. *The World Without Us*. New York: Picador, 2007.